What Others Are Saying About Coach-Ability and The Tricycle Effect

While in the USAF, I was fortunate enough to serve my country from the White House to the mountain-top communications sites in Europe and Eurasia and across the great U.S. for more than two decades. Following my retirement from the USAF, I spent another two decades working in the space and intelligence communities. In both arenas, inspiring people and getting them to realize their potential was a must in order to accomplish the mission. I met Dane toward the end of my military career when he was a young Captain in Turkey assigned to what became one of the largest Groups in the USAF. From the very first day I met him, his character and willingness to take on any task was evident. Not only was he far more capable than many officers above his rank, I saw he had the unique ability to inspire those both above and below his rank. Over the next two years as we served together, Dane brought not only good ideas to the newly formed organization from himself, he encouraged and motivated his staff to do the same. His leadership skills helped mold the organization and as a mentor he set the example for his younger people to follow. As a result, and I attribute so much of this to Dane, the Group received the prestigious McClellan Award for the best large communications group in the USAF after our first two years. I've always considered him to be the best young leader that I have ever known and the AF lost one of its very best when he moved back into civilian life. That's why I was so excited to find that he had put his remarkable leadership skills into print. I enjoyed reading this most recent of Dane's books and I know that it will accomplish its purpose. Dane touches on so many good points and makes them very easy to visualize. I am proud and honored to endorse his new book and hope that you, as the reader, will adopt these ideas. I am also hopeful, with God's help, that you continue to develop and improve your character! You can't change your personality but we all should work on improving our "character" to be one that motivates, listens, respects and accepts those around us. If you do, you can't help but be a success!! Trike on!

— James G. Whited Col. USAF (Ret)
VP Intelligence & Space Systems (C4 Systems) General Dynamics (Ret)

The lessons that Dane teaches in Coach-Ability and The Tricycle Effect will impact you and transform the lives of those you are working to influence as a leader and coach. It's a call to action to cultivate our character skills, by self-coaching, coaching others, and being coached by other leaders and mentors. His stories and Chalk Talk Coaching Tips are so powerful. Everyone in your sphere of influence needs this book!

— Tim Novak
Maxwell Leadership certified speaker, coach, trainer, author

The Coach-Ability and The Tricycle Effect is an essential read for anyone aspiring to leadership or leaders committed to personal growth. This book places a strong emphasis on coaching character, highlighting it as the foundational element for individual development.

The strategic use of design callouts effectively illuminates key topics, complemented by comprehensive worksheets at the end of each chapter that encourage thorough review and meaningful reflection.

The triad of coachability introduced in the book guides readers through a transformative journey, starting with self-coaching, progressing to coaching others, and embracing being coached by others. This progression mirrors the mastery of self, the act of helping others grow, and the continuous learning that comes from being open to mentorship.

Through engaging storytelling, the book vividly brings this journey to life, reinforcing crucial lessons and facilitating deep learning. It serves as a roadmap for anyone striving to become better leaders by focusing on character development and embracing a coachable mindset.

Well done Dane!

— Will Lukang, Creator of the IWillAim Program
Speaker, Coach, and Trainer

Look at any successful leader and you'll see a powerful principle at work. We can only go as high and as far as the caliber of coaches in our lives. In Dane's comprehensive book, discover how to increase your Coach-Ability and create the life of your dreams.
— Dr. Kary Oberbrunner, WSJ and USA Today bestselling author of 14 books
CEO of Igniting Souls® and Instant IP™

Just finished reading Dane Deutsch's new book Coach-Ability and The Tricycle Effect. When I started this book I felt that it might be a book for just coaches but I was wrong. The more I got into the book I realized that the Coach-Ability concept he was promoting applied not just for coaches but for anyone who wanted to improve themselves, their families and help those around them. The different life experiences that he had and shares in the book make the reader feel more like a companion on the journey instead of a bystander. I would recommend this book to anyone who is searching for a way to make their life and the lives of others better.
— Doug Peterson
Retired Teacher of 42 years

Dane Deutsch is not just an author, he is an example of what he writes. I have had the privilege to get to work with Dane through the process of publishing two of his books. I have watched as he put the principles in place not just for a stage presentation but in real life. In his new book Coach-Ability and The Tricycle Effect you are going to find principles for life and leadership that are essential to function in a world that is fractured by organizational distrust and individual failures. This book may be the difference between you merely being 'successful' by the world's standards or leaving a legacy that endures for generations to come.

— Tony Colson, DMin
Owner, GreatnessMakers.com, Pastor at ICON Church

Dane's book is an inspiring and insightful guide to leadership rooted in character. As an Air Force officer veteran, entrepreneur, and leadership coach, he brings a wealth of experience to the table, illustrating how integrity, humility, and accountability are crucial for personal and professional growth. Through engaging stories and practical advice, Dane challenges readers to cultivate coach-ability and lead with their character at the forefront. This is a must-read for anyone looking to develop themselves as a leader and make a meaningful impact in the lives of others. Trike on!

— Lloyd Erlemann
CEO - Kairos Executive Programs

Dane has done it again! The tricycle image is the perfect analogy that reveals how character, competence, and courage work together to increase one's influence with others. Now, Dane offers a model of coachability that will help us not only coach the character of others but also be coached by others and coach ourselves. If you grow your coachability, you will grow your influence."

— Perry Holley | Sr. Facilitator & Executive Coach
MAXWELL LEADERSHIP

"I am a big fan of leadership coaching and even a bigger fan of coaching character. Dane's coachability model, paired with the Tricycle Effect components of character, competence, and courage, is a winning combination for leaders at all levels."

– Chris Goede | Executive Vice President
MAXWELL LEADERSHIP

Dane Deutsch has been a professional friend for more than twenty years. In our service and leadership in the military, we both learned that Character and Courage were the foundation for achieving the Technical Mission and serving the People. His Tricycle Effect has been a brilliant way to illustrate that concept. In this new book, Dane has provided Coach-Ability, the most important thing anyone needs to learn and apply. The ability to self-coach is the only way we can consistently grow as a person and a leader, and this book provides amazing stories and coaching to help us all develop. Even as a senior leader, this book is helping me coach myself to keep growing. I know it will do the same for you.

— Leon "Lee" Ellis, CSP
Colonel USAF (Ret.)
President, Leadership Freedom LLC (dba Leading with Honor)

I've had the distinct pleasure of working alongside Dane through Maxwell Leadership, and I can say without hesitation that he is a true embodiment of character and leadership. Dane is not only a man of integrity but also a remarkable coach who leads with unwavering conviction and empathy. His ability to inspire and guide others is a testament to his deep commitment to personal and professional growth.

Dane's book, Coach-Ability and the Tricycle Effect, is a powerful reflection of the wisdom and character that he brings to every interaction. It's more than just a book—it's a transformative guide that places character at the heart of leadership. Through engaging storytelling and practical exercises, Dane leads readers on a journey to develop not only their leadership skills but also their character, which is the foundation of true success.

I particularly admire the way Dane embodies servant leadership, as highlighted in his story of his teammates sacrificing their personal goals to save a life during a challenging climb. This mirrors the values I hold dear in my own journey—putting others first, even at the expense of personal gains, to truly lead with integrity and compassion.

Additionally, Dane's emphasis on self-coaching and mental resilience resonates deeply with my own experiences. Like Dane, I believe that overcoming challenges begins within, and his insights into transforming internal hurdles into growth opportunities are invaluable.

Whether you're seeking to enhance your leadership skills, navigate life's challenges, or grow personally and professionally, Dane's insights in this book are invaluable. He is a leader in every sense of the word, and I am honored to call him a friend and colleague.

— Michael J Pope Jr
CEO of Michael Pope Training, LLC
Executive Director Maxwell Leadership & Neuroencoding Specialist

Leadership books can't just be interesting – they have to be useful. Fortunately, Coach-Ability and the Tricycle effect is both. Dane's background in the military combined with his years as a gymnastics coach give him a wealth of relevant stories that reveal how the character of leadership drives impact and results. Better yet, he provides the frameworks and practical tips to become aware of the power of your character and how to leverage it for the benefit of your people, your organization, and the communities you serve.

— Kelly Kiel Garramone, CEO, KRW International, Return on Character®

Dane Deutsch's book is a much-needed guide for cultivating the strong character and self-awareness that our self-centered and polarized societies around the world desperately need. In an era where personal development often seems disconnected from service, this book masterfully bridges that gap by illustrating how genuine growth begins with coaching oneself, coaching others, and being open to receiving guidance. Dane's exploration of "coach-ability" delves deeply into the mechanics of personal and professional growth, emphasizing the importance of humility, character, and trust. Through thought-provoking analogies such as the Tricycle Effect from his first book and practical workbook exercises, readers are encouraged to reflect on how character drives actions and decisions, shaping not only individual leadership but also the way we influence those around us.

As Viktor Frankl highlighted the will to meaning as life's driving force, Dane illustrates how coach-ability is crucial in our search for purpose. With each chapter, the reader is guided through the importance of self-coaching, being open to feedback, and fostering relationships built on trust and integrity. His focus on character-driven leadership, illustrated through real-life examples and reflective exercises, reminds us that growth is not an isolated process but one grounded in service to others.

This book is a powerful call to embrace humility, resilience, and continuous self-improvement as essential components of leadership and personal fulfillment, making it a must-read for anyone striving to navigate life's challenges with character and purpose.

— Dr. Saltuk Karahan
Undergraduate Program Director, School of Cybersecurity
Old Dominion University
Former Turkish NATO Officer (Colonel)

This book is a must read! I love the stories Dane shares from his personal life. They highlight the various themes of the book, the main one being character is the key. The stories also make this book so readable, and keeps the reader intrigued and wanting to read and learn more.

COACH-ABILITY AND THE TRICYCLE EFFECT shares Dane's exciting and challenging life journey. The book is a roadmap for success, and demonstrates how to climb the mountains we find before us.

I especially love the Chalk Talks and the Workbooks which emphasize the application of the knowledge presented, because without application no real learning takes place.

Learn how being coachable and coaching others is not only for leaders, but for EVERYONE as they seek a significant life with meaning and purpose.

— Guy Doud
National Teacher of the Year – 1986
Motivational Speaker & Author – Molder of Dreams (Focus on the Family Publishing)

Coach-Ability
and
The Tricycle Effect™

COACHING CHARACTER *as*
the FOUNDATION OF LEADERSHIP

Coach-Ability
and
The Tricycle Effect™

COACHING CHARACTER *as*
the FOUNDATION OF LEADERSHIP

Dane A. Deutsch

Foreword by Tom Ziglar

Coach-Ability and The Tricyle Effect™ © 2024 by Dane A. Deutsch. All rights reserved.

Published by Author Academy Elite
PO Box 43, Powell, OH 43065

www.AuthorAcademyElite.com

All rights reserved. This book contains material protected under international and federal copyright laws and treaties. Any unauthorized reprint or use of this material is prohibited. No part of this book may be reproduced or transmitted in any form or by any means, electronic or mechanical, including photocopying, recording, or by any information storage and retrieval system, without express written permission from the author.

Identifiers:
LCCN: **2024902353**
ISBN: 979-8-88583-330-1 (paperback)
ISBN: 979-8-88583-331-8 (hardback)
ISBN: 979-8-88583-332-5 (ebook)

Available in paperback, hardback, audiobook, and e-book

All Scripture quotations, unless otherwise indicated, are taken from the Holy Bible, New International Version®, NIV®. Copyright ©1973, 1978, 1984, 2011 by Biblica, Inc.™ Used by permission of Zondervan. All rights reserved worldwide. www.zondervan.com The "NIV" and "New International Version" are trademarks registered in the United States Patent and Trademark Office by Biblica, Inc.™

Any Internet addresses (websites, blogs, etc.) and telephone numbers printed in this book are offered as a resource. They are not intended in any way to be or imply an endorsement by Author Academy Elite, nor does Author Academy Elite vouch for the content of these sites and numbers for the life of this book.

Dedication

To my pa, Cecil Deutsch

I joyfully dedicate this book to my pa, a man of boundless love, character, and tremendous wisdom.

Pa, you've always been a haven of support and a beacon of strength in my life. Your kindness, deep care, and thoughtfulness about the friendships and relationships in your life have always been apparent. Your father, a veteran of World War I, shaped you, just as your experiences as a Korean War vet shaped me, even though my military service was in the Middle Eastern theater during peacetime.

Your belief that you were put on this earth with a purpose, to nurture and guide my sister and me, has been a light guiding my journey. Regardless of what you did, your actions were always leading with character first, tailored to add value and make a difference in our lives. From being a steadfast presence at my sporting events to helping me navigate through my endeavors in Scouting, the military, and in business, your support was unwavering. You weren't just my dad—you were a role model for me as well.

When I became an AAU state wrestling champion in Minnesota at 145 pounds, I saw your pride, and it fueled me. My journey through Boy Scouts, from Eagle to Vigil, was to make you proud, just as you were making me proud by exploring the Scouting world alongside me, eventually earning brotherhood in the Order of the Arrow.

Choosing to follow in your footsteps, I ventured into the Air Force after college, serving nearly eight years of active duty, with five of those years and three tours of duty overseas in Turkey. I remember the joy when you visited me and our family twice, flying on C-130s, using the perks of your retired status. Your stories of flying and learning from pilots, even as you, a master sergeant and one of the Air Force's first jet mechanics, worked diligently, were incredibly inspiring.

Dane and his Pa

Many lessons you bestowed upon me were not derived from schools, Scouts, or other leaders but were heartfelt insights directly from you over many coffee times at McDonald's. Your leadership, always prioritizing character first, shone brightly through attributes like responsibility, trustworthiness, respect, fairness, kindness, caring, loyalty, and integrity.

In business and in life, you were there, guiding me in principle and character values. So, I dedicate this book to you, Dad, to honor the leadership and character you seamlessly exemplified. Your teachings and love continue to guide me, and for that, I'm endlessly grateful.

Thank you, Pa!

Contents

Author's Note	1
Foreword	5
Prologue	7
Part 1: We Define Coach-Ability	11
1. Introduction	13
Workbook for Coach-Ability, Chapter 1	19
2. Review of the Tricycle Effect	21
Workbook for Coach-Ability, Chapter 2	29
3. The Definition of Coach-Ability	31
Workbook for Coach-Ability, Chapter 3	51
4. Signs of Coach-Ability	53
Workbook for Coach-Ability, Chapter 4	75
5. The Benefits of Coach-Ability—Coach-Leader	77
Workbook for Coach-Ability, Chapter 5	99
Part 2: Coaching Yourself	101
6. How to Develop Coach-Ability	103

Workbook for Coach-Ability, Chapter 6	131
7. Barriers to Coach-Ability	135
Workbook for Coach-Ability, Chapter 7	155
8. How to Overcome Barriers to Coach-Ability	159
Workbook for Coach-Ability, Chapter 8	185
9. Coach-Ability in Personal Life	189
Workbook for Coach-Ability, Chapter 9	203
Part 3: Coaching Others	205
10. Coaching and Mentorship for Developing Coach-Ability	207
Workbook for Coach-Ability, Chapter 10	223
11. How to Encourage Coach-Ability in Others	225
Workbook for Coach-Ability, Chapter 11	249
12. Coach-Ability in Leadership	251
Workbook for Coach-Ability, Chapter 12	271
Part 4: Others Coach Us—Examples in Real Life	273
13. The Importance of Character in Leadership	275
Workbook for Coach-Ability, Chapter 13	281
14. Your Word Is Your Bond: A Lesson in Integrity and Commitment	283
Workbook for Coach-Ability, Chapter 14	289

15. Cultivating Positive Mindsets Through Humility and Mentorship	293
Workbook for Coach-Ability, Chapter 15	299
16. Pressure Always Reveals True Character, and Then We Can Be Mentored	301
Workbook for Coach-Ability, Chapter 16	307
Conclusion	311
Epilogue	315
Coach-Ability Workbook Chapter Fill-in-the-Blanks Answer Key	319
Resource and Reference List	331
Endnotes	337

Author's Note

Dear aspiring coach-able leader,

If you're holding this note, you're not just starting to read another book—you're stepping into a realm where personal growth and leadership transcend mere concepts and theories. *Coach-Ability and the Tricycle Effect* is not a work of fiction or a collection of untested ideas. It is the crystallization of who I am, Coach Dane, pouring myself into your life through these practical pages that pulse with the lifeblood of practical experience.

This book is my open heart—a treasure trove of wisdom I learned from being coach-able and knowledge from other coaches and mentors in the trenches of life's most challenging climbs and exhilarating peaks. Every word is rooted in the rich soil of real-world struggles and triumphs. It's for you, on your journey to success, to learn deep down that true significance lies in leading with character first and adding significance for others in serving them for the greater good.

I invite you to journey with me through stories that teem with life, lessons that I experienced, lived, and learned, and strategies tested in the crucibles of both personal trials, team experiences, and leadership triumphs. This book is not an academic exercise—it's a personal conversation between me and you, along with my coaching and mentorship for you in ink and passion.

Within these pages, I aim to inspire you and coach you into an arena where character is not just a word but the core of your being so you can be a champion of character. In this book, *coach-able* is not just a catchy term—it's a way of life, a conscious choice to absorb the wisdom of growing and developing your character skills while simultaneously offering your unique coaching insights and values to make a difference for others.

I've woven my life's fabric of experiences into this work so that you can grasp the tangible threads of coach-ability and weave them into your own life's tapestry of success and significance. With every chapter, every anecdote, and every challenge, I'm right there with you, coaching you to pedal harder, climb higher, and lead better with character first.

Coach Dane on Peak of Mt. Ararat at 17,000ft.

AUTHOR'S NOTE

Coach-Ability and the Tricycle Effect is your invitation to transform and grow as a coach-leader. It's your call to action to cultivate your character skills—not someday but starting now. This is your playbook for becoming a person of influence, a beacon of inspiration in serving others, and a catalyst for positive change in both your life and the lives of those around you that you touch every day.

Remember, this is not about lofty ideals. It's about the daily grind, the small decisions, the tiny character habits you form, and the values you uphold. It's about being honest with where you're at and taking intentional steps toward where you want to be. It's about not just doing things right but doing the right things.

As you turn each page, I encourage you to not just read but to engage fully. Let each lesson challenge you, and practice the action steps at the end of each chapter. Let each story I share inspire and motivate you, and let each exercise transform you. Apply these values and watch as the principles of *Coach-Ability and the Tricycle Effect* take hold of your life and move you forward in ways you never imagined possible. Most importantly, you will learn that you can do more than *leave* a legacy—you can *live* your legacy now.

This book is your road map and compass to help you navigate and learn to be coach-able, to lead with character first, and to understand that the true measure of success is the significance you add to the lives of others.

So, my friend, are you ready to begin the journey of *Coach-Ability and the Tricycle Effect* through authentic character-driven personal and professional leadership growth? Let's get trikin'!

Trike on,

Coach Dane

Your coach on this journey of greatness

Foreword

by Tom Ziglar

I AM FREQUENTLY ASKED *Will you coach me?* I love to coach, but I have to say that results vary. Why?

I believe much of it boils down to *coach-ability*—meaning the individual also needs to be prepared to be coached. In his new book, Dane Deutsch makes a compelling case for the value of mentally preparing for the coaching experience by establishing a foundation of high moral character.

My dad, Zig Ziglar, always said, "The number one reason for my success is my character and integrity." I love how Dane has built his whole platform on that foundation. It's about character and integrity.

What an incredible difference we would see in our society—and world—if leaders, coaches, and mentors focused on producing and developing solid character in their learners. With the right character and virtue, the right things are done in the right way.

I find it especially encouraging to read this book, presenting the teaching and instilling the eternal values of respect and character. Dane offers a particularly fascinating tie-in of mental preparation for coaching (i.e., "prepare to be coach-able," which, in and of itself, may be both unique and fulfilling) with the establishment and development of character that leads to a solid foundation for setting and reaching goals, both personally and professionally.

Coach-Ability is a great guide and asset for anyone who wants to build their life on the foundation of character. If you are ready to coach yourself and someone else to both success and significance, get your pen handy as you devour this book!

— Tom Ziglar

Proud son of Zig Ziglar and president and CEO of Ziglar, Inc.

Prologue

HAVE YOU EVER FELT stuck in your personal or professional life, unsure of how to move forward or make positive changes? If so, you're not alone. Many people struggle to achieve their goals and fulfill their potential, whether it's in their careers, relationships, or personal life.

The good news is that there is a skill—in fact, a key competence skill—that can help individuals set goals and unlock obstacles and challenges to achieve personal and professional leadership growth. That secret is a people skill called coach-ability. In this book, I'm going to coach you on how to become coach-able.

Being coach-able means being open to feedback, learning from experiences, and making positive changes to achieve personal and professional growth. It can help you be successful, but even more importantly, it can make you significant to yourself and others. Coach-ability is a critical trait that can lead to personal and professional success. It is the ability to be open to feedback, willing to always be learning, and embrace a growth mindset.

Ever heard someone say they wanted to leave a legacy? By the time we finish this book together, I want you to know you can leave a legacy, because you lived a legacy. Being coach-able ensures you will live your legacy now.

This book is a comprehensive, four-part guide to coach-ability:

- Part 1: We review *the Tricycle Effect*™ and the definition of coach-ability, including the benefits of being coach-able and how to develop coach-ability.

- Part 2: We discuss the importance of self-coaching.

- Part 3: We explore how we can learn to coach others.

- Part 4: We learn how to open ourselves and be coached by others.

Together, these sections explore coach-ability from different perspectives or angles, and we learn what it truly means to be coach-able.

In each chapter, I share stories that help you learn the need and importance of coach-ability to get connected and stay connected to other people in this tumultuous and exponentially technological and fast-changing world we live in. You will learn practical tips, strategies, and insights, and this book will guide you on your journey toward developing this essential people skill, one of the tricycle's competence wheels in the back. At the end of each chapter, I have a short "chalk talk" to review the key points and give you a suggested action step with the opportunity to develop a strategy and direction for moving forward.

In addition, after each Chalk Talk Coaching Tip, there is also an opportunity to test your knowledge and understanding of what you just read. Each chapter includes three Fill-in-the-Blanks questions as well as three Reflective Questions for you to self-examine and develop a plan to encourage character skills and leadership growth and development.

Whether you're looking to improve your performance at work, build stronger relationships with others, grow a stronger marriage, or achieve personal growth and self-improvement, coach-ability is an essential trait that can help you unlock your full potential by growing from success to significance.

Trike on!

Part 1:

We Define Coach-Ability

CHAPTER 1
Introduction

Leadership is influence, nothing more and nothing less. — John C. Maxwell[1]

WELCOME TO THE JOURNEY of coach-ability! In this book, we're diving deep into a vital concept that pivots on a triad of ways to be coach-able:

- Coaching yourself

- Coaching others

- Being coached by others

Most of the time, people discuss and explore coaching as if it is only on the outside of who they are. There's a twist, however, that many of us seldom consider. It's a third, and equally crucial side of coaching: *coaching yourself*.

> **Challenge/Problem statement:** Self-coaching is often an overlooked aspect of personal development, leading to missed opportunities for self-improvement and influence.

This triad of elements (i.e., self-coaching, coaching others, and being coached by others) creates a habit where coaching begins with the self, then ripples out to coach others, and finally, invites coaching from others.

It is important to understand that self-coaching is inherently woven together with our coaching of others and our being coached by others. Self-coaching, you could say, is happening all the time and in every thought we have. In other words, each part of the triad does not simply stand alone. After all, we are humans and everything we do is a result of integration, and life coach-ability is the thread that connects and brings all legs of the triad together.

As an example, when I am coaching a gymnast, I must coach their self-talk as much as their technical skill. Otherwise, optimal progress might not be made because of many things I may not know about and cannot see directly. There are many factors that are unseen and are in the gymnast's head that can be related to self-talk, such as fear, uncertainty, lack of trust in the coach, lack of belief in self, lying to self, and more. From my experiences being a coach for thousands of athletes, I found that if I listened well, I could take the gymnast's feedback (spoken or unspoken) and improve my coaching ability going forward. In other words, even one of my preschoolers, through a mistake, might coach me on something I could use for my advanced gymnasts.

A perfect example of this occurred when I was coaching one of my gymnasts on a skill for high bar. She could do the skill perfectly all by herself as long as I was standing next to her on a box at that height. I did that for weeks, and then one night, I asked why she didn't believe she could complete the skill by herself.

Her response was remarkable. She shouted back at me, "Because that would be a lie!"

I had never thought that since she did not yet "own" the skill, she might actually consider what I was asking her to do as a lie. I heard her loud and clear, and then I knew how to coach her through that. She coached me on how to address what she was battling in her mind, and within the next two weeks, I was standing below the bar, watching her do some of the most beautiful skills all by herself.

Some in the business profession might consider this example by another, and perhaps more familiar, term: impostor syndrome. So, as you can see, whether in sports or business, self-talk, coaching others, and being coached by others (maybe even one of your own athletes, employees, or teammates) are all integrated, and we have to allow coach-ability to happen in all legs of the triad.

Each of us talks to ourselves more than anyone else day-to-day. Have you ever thought about that? We average 16,000 words per day when we speak out loud, but we speak even faster when we talk to ourselves. Most of us even spend a great deal of time speaking to ourselves in images or visualizations that can represent thousands of words without a single word spoken (externally or internally).[2] I often share that if a picture is worth a thousand words, then a video is worth 10,000 words or more. It goes beyond that too.

For instance, sometimes fear is not just spoken in words but in feelings and emotions too. So what I call the theater in our mind runs continually in thoughts and emotions and is the most important person to coach of all. We all practice it—we just don't know it. Most likely, most of us haven't really given it much thought. Some people simply call our self-talk or self-coaching something like focus, daydreaming, or simply visualization.

Internal communication with ourselves happens constantly throughout the day. That means we are also our most influential coach. Some people simply refer to this as self-talk, but others call it the inner critic or inner voice. So self-talk with the inner voice is the voice that takes up most of our time and attention throughout each day.

Being coach-able essentially means aspiring to be a better leader. As John C. Maxwell puts it, "Leadership is influence—nothing more, nothing less."[3]

Leadership transcends titles, positions, and formal authority. Sometimes the person who leads from the bottom or the individual who speaks the least affects and influences a team or group the most. But again, the person who influences us the most is ourselves, so being coach-able means that you must first be coach-able and loyal by influencing yourself through your own voices, pictures, dreams, goals, and desires.

Let me remind you from my first book, *The Tricycle Effect*, that we "lead people and manage things."[4] By *things*, we mean systems, processes, procedures, money, etc. Or, as Maxwell might say, we influence people and manage things.

During this coach-ability study, we will home in on character-driven values leadership.

By embedding character into everything we do, we enhance our ability to coach ourselves and steer our influence in a positive direction.

Billy Graham said, "Integrity is the glue that holds our way of life together....When wealth is lost, nothing is lost; when health is lost, something is lost; when the character is lost, all is lost."[5]

Consequently, our behavior and posture—our lived examples—will sculpt a path for ourselves and others, positioning us to effectively coach when the opportunity or *character-coaching moments* arise.

Equally, rooting ourselves in character enables the humility, vulnerability, transparency, and accountability needed to be self-coach-able and remain coach-able by others even if others do not realize their coaching or influence on us.

Your leadership, your influence over self and with others, has the potential to reshape your life and the lives of others. This will encourage them to perceive life not merely as a quest for success but as a journey toward adding value to others, making a difference, and ultimately, living a life of significance by becoming significant to themselves and others.

Chalk Talk Coaching Tip

Coach-ability emphasizes a crucial coaching trio: self-coaching, coaching others, and receiving coaching, illustrating how these elements are interconnected to enhance personal growth and leadership. This approach encourages a mindset of continuous self-improvement and the ability to positively influence others through our actions and character.

- **Promise of solution:** Integrating self-coaching into your daily routine can significantly enhance personal growth and the ability to positively influence both yourself and others.

- **Suggested action step**: Begin a daily practice of self-reflection, and identify one area of your personal or professional life that you wish to improve. Spend at least 15 minutes focusing on how you can coach yourself to develop in this area, and consider how it will also benefit those around you.

Workbook for Coach-Ability, Chapter 1

INTRODUCTION

Fill-in-the-Blanks

1. "Leadership is _____, nothing more, nothing less." — John C. Maxwell

2. The triad of coach-ability consists of coaching _____, coaching others, and being coached by others.

3. Being coach-able means aspiring to be a better leader, influencing ourselves through our own voices, pictures, dreams, goals, and _____.

Reflective Questions

1. Reflect on a time when self-coaching helped you overcome a personal challenge. What was the situation, and how did coaching yourself change the outcome?

2. Think about a moment when you were coaching

someone else. What did you learn about your own coaching style, and how did it affect the person you were coaching?

3. Recall a time when being coached by someone else led to a significant insight or improvement in your life or work. What was the feedback or advice, and why was it so influential for you?

Please take your time to thoughtfully fill in the blanks and reflect on the questions above. These exercises are designed to deepen your understanding of the coach-ability concept and how it applies to your life and leadership journey.

Summary of Chapter 1 Workbook

Chapter 1 introduces the foundational concept of coach-ability, emphasizing the importance of the triad, which includes self-coaching, coaching others, and being receptive to coaching from others. This chapter sets the stage for understanding that coaching is not just an external influence but also an internal dialogue that continuously shapes our thoughts and actions. The workbook is designed to encourage readers to examine how self-coaching affects personal development, consider the impact of coaching others, and recognize the value of openness to being coached. Reflective questions prompt readers to think about their self-talk, the learning they have gained from coaching others, and the personal insights gained from being coached, tying these experiences back to their leadership and influence.

Chapter 2
Review of the Tricycle Effect

Talent is a gift, but character is a choice.
— John C. Maxwell[1]

Before we dive into *Coach-Ability and the Tricycle Effect*, let's revisit the fundamental concept of the Tricycle Effect. My aim has always been to keep things simple and relatable. To do that, I provide an image—the tricycle—that sticks in your mind and is something you can easily recall and build upon since most of us have ridden tricycles and Big Wheels at some point in our lives when we were kids.

Per ChatGPT version 4.0, "It is interesting that the word *character* can metaphorically reflect a mark or imprint, especially when referring to a person's qualities, virtues, or moral values. A person's character is often considered the sum of their habitual actions, values, and thoughts, which together leave a mark on their behavior and interactions with others. This 'imprint' can influence how others perceive and interact with them. The concept of character implies a degree of permanence or stability in a person's behavior and moral compass, similar to how a mark or imprint suggests a lasting impression."[7]

Now, let's talk about something I always love to share: Adults are essentially just big kids. What personality did you display at age three? Well, that's still embedded within you. But your character, which encompasses your values and character-istics developed through experiences and training, evolves over time and can even influence your own personality.

Here's some good news: your personality is not going to change much, but your character can be developed. Or as I like to say, "Character skills can grow."

Your character is not set in stone like some things in life. Traits like caring, respect, and empathy can absolutely be developed with goals, priorities, time, and conscious effort. Character skills can become productive habits for us. So, nurturing our character skills is a crucial part of our maturity and journey as "human becomings."

> **Challenge/Problem statement**: Although our innate personality traits are deeply embedded from a young age, developing a strong, virtuous character is often overlooked as a dynamic, lifelong process.

I've always emphasized the term *human becomings* to my athletes and students. We're not static human *beings*. We are not just in a state of being. We're dynamic, ever-evolving human becomings, continually growing and morphing in life and developing, hopefully with character-istics that mold us and shape us into champions of character.

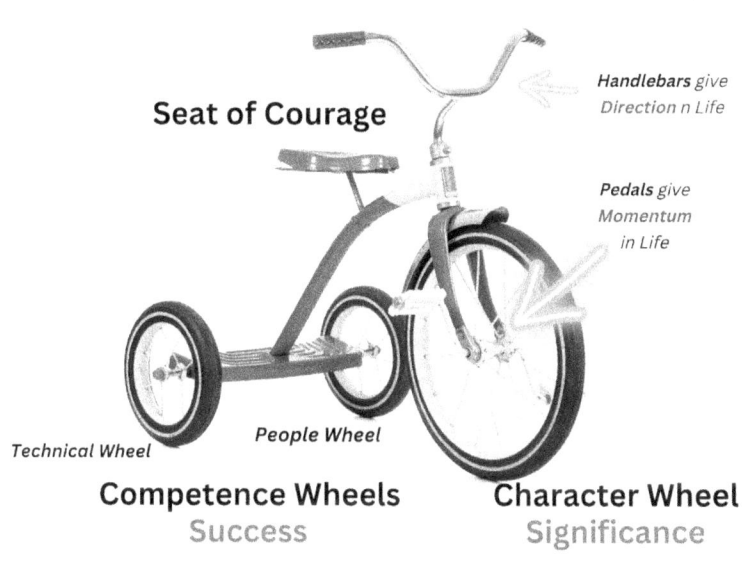

Why the tricycle image? you may ask. As I share, almost every one of us has ridden a tricycle or a Big Wheel during our childhood. Picture this: The largest wheel on a trike is the front wheel, which I dub the character skills wheel. It has spokes on the wheel that represent values and character-istics such as trustworthiness, respect, responsibility, fairness, caring, loyalty, empathy, kindness, integrity, and many more. I like to call these character skills.

Meanwhile, the two smaller rear wheels I call the competence skills wheels. These represent the technical skills and people skills wheels, respectively.

Technical skills comprise tangible technical abilities and wheel spokes, which are any talents and skills that can be learned, like typing, repairing an engine, playing an instrument, baking a cake, or riding a tricycle. You get the idea.

People skills spokes encapsulate skills required to work and play with other people, and they are skills that can be learned as well, such as teamwork, leadership, communication, problem-solving, and critical thinking. Ideally, the competence skills wheels are balanced and roughly equal in size, whereas the character skills wheel dominates as the *biggest* wheel, located in the front of the tricycle (trike) and leads the way.

Sitting atop the tricycle is the seat, and I call that the seat of courage. This seat represents the courage and boldness of the driver or rider to make the right choices and decisions at the right times and for the right reasons.

The individual sitting in the seat holds the handlebars (connected directly to the character skills wheel) and controls the pedals (also linked directly to the character skills wheel). Your character (who you are in the seat of courage) influences your life's direction and momentum via these handlebars and pedals, shaping the results of every decision you make from that seat of courage.

Essentially, you get your direction and momentum in life from your character skills wheel. As John C. Maxwell says, "Talent is a gift, but character is a choice."[8] If character is a choice, then we can choose to work on, grow, and develop our character skills.

As a further reference, the character wheel is what I label the character quotient wheel. The two competence wheels are the intelligence quotient wheels. And that vital seat of courage? I refer to it as the emotional quotient because many decisions arise from our emotions. It's crucial to acknowledge that although our feelings might not always guide us to the right decision, they undeniably highlight our inherent human nature and continual growth in the decisions we make to grow our character skills and move ahead through all of life's experiences as human becomings.

With that refresher and understanding, I'm eager to journey through the next step of this book with you and define coach-ability. Keep rolling forward, team, and as always, trike on!

Video Explanation of The Tricycle Effect (TTE) with a Doodly

Chalk Talk Coaching Tip

In the Tricycle Effect, character is the front wheel of the trike—our character skills wheel—leading us in life and showcasing values such as trust and integrity. The two smaller back wheels—our competence skills wheels for technical and people skills—support us, but it's the courageous choices we make in the seat to grow our character that truly drive us forward as human becomings.

- **Promise of solution**: Acknowledging that character is not fixed but can be shaped and strengthened through intentional effort, individuals can transform their innate personality traits into mature and robust character traits over time.

- **Suggested action step**: Identify and focus on one character skill each week, such as empathy or respect. Actively seek out situations to practice this skill, reflect on your experiences, and note progress and areas for improvement in a character development journal.

This focused effort encourages ongoing personal growth and the embodiment of a character that influences and inspires.

Workbook for Coach-Ability, Chapter 2

Review of the Tricycle Effect

Fill-in-the-Blanks

1. The front wheel of the tricycle, dubbed the character skills wheel, includes spokes that are values and character-istics such as trustworthiness, respect, and _____.

2. The two smaller rear wheels, known as the competence skills wheels, represent the technical skills and _____ skills wheels, respectively.

3. Sitting atop the tricycle is the seat of _____, which represents the courage to make the right choices and decisions.

Reflective Questions

1. Reflect on your own character skills wheel. Which values or character-istics do you feel are your strongest spokes, and why do you value them so highly?

2. Considering the competence skills wheels, how do you balance improving your technical skills with enhancing your people skills, and which area do you find more challenging to develop?

3. Describe a time when you had to sit in the seat of courage. What difficult choice or decision did you face, and how did you rely on your character to guide you?

Take a moment to fill in the blanks and reflect on these questions. They are designed to help you think deeply about your own character and competence and how they influence your journey through life as a human becoming.

Summary of Chapter 2 Workbook

Chapter 2 emphasizes the Tricycle Effect where character leads as the front wheel, signifying its paramount role in driving our actions and decisions, with trustworthiness, respect, and kindness as key components. The rear wheels symbolize the technical and people skills that support us, but it's the seat of courage where decisions are made, reflecting our willingness to make the right choices. This analogy draws a clear picture of how character, competence, and courage work together, illustrating that character isn't fixed but can be developed like a muscle, influencing our professional and personal growth. The workbook questions invite reflection on the reader's own character strengths, challenges in developing competence skills, and moments when courage played a significant role in decision-making.

Chapter 3
The Definition of Coach-Ability

Attitude is a reflection of character and character is a reflection of habit. — Tom Ziglar[9]

Ability to Coach and Be Coached = Coach-Able

IN THIS CHAPTER, WE will define *coach-ability* and why it is essential for personal and professional growth. We will also provide an overview of the book and what readers can expect to learn.

1. Definition of *Coach-Ability*

Coach-ability is the ability to be open to feedback, learn from experiences, and make positive changes to achieve personal and professional growth. Being coach-able involves being receptive to constructive criticism, willing to learn and try new things, and having a growth mindset in all three ways of the coach-ability triad: self, others, and by others.

2. Why Coach-Ability Is Important for Personal and Professional Growth

Coach-ability is important for personal and professional growth for several reasons. Being coach-able can help you identify areas for improvement and develop new skills and strategies. Being coach-able can also help you adapt to make changes and adapt to new challenges in the workplace or in your personal life, which can lead to improved outcomes and success, and thereby joy and fulfillment in life.

> Challenge/Problem statement: Many people struggle to embrace coach-ability, often missing the opportunity to grow personally and professionally due to a lack of openness to feedback and new experiences.

In the realm of coach-ability, we don't only aim to influence others when we coach them, but we also embark on a journey of self-influence, and many times, we learn to coach ourselves much better by coaching others. Ask yourself, How do I influence myself? What does my self-talk sound like? How does my body language fuel my self-talk?

Moreover, once we've understood and harnessed these aspects in ourselves, how do they permit us to coach others effectively? These questions are fundamental and form the backbone of our journey through this book, aptly titled *Coach-Ability and the Tricycle Effect*.

Let me share with you a story that reflects this idea of coach-ability. This story is a little long, but it encompasses and illustrates coach-ability perfectly. I promise you the story will provide real context and meaning for you.

This story took place in the late 1980s when I climbed Mount Ararat. Mt. Ararat is a 17,000-foot mountain located in the far eastern side of Turkey. In Turkish, it's called Agridag. Agri means pain, and Dag means mountain. Therefore, Mt. Ararat, Agridag in Turkish, is really the mountain of pain.[10] Ararat is a very dangerous mountain.

Mt Ararat - 17,000ft Mountain

A lot of people have climbed this mountain looking for Noah's Ark, including James Irwin, who was one of the astronauts who flew to the moon. On one of his climbs, astronaut James Irwin was injured when he fell on Mt. Ararat while searching for Noah's Ark.

Sometimes, you could have a clear blue day with no clouds in the sky, and in a matter of seconds, clouds encircle the peak of the mountain, and really dangerous lightning occurs. Mt. Ararat is also an extinct volcano with lots of volcanic ash on the surface. Anytime you take a step, you might take one step forward and then slide back three or four feet. So, sometimes it's pretty hard climbing, and that only adds to how dangerous climbing up Mt. Ararat can be.

One year, the local tourism agency at Incirlik Air Base in Adana, Turkey, decided to offer a "hike" up Mt. Ararat. As it turned out, we had 12 to 15 people sign up who wanted to climb to the peak, which is 17,000 feet high. The local Turkish tourism company we signed up with did a great job of marketing and sales by getting us to believe it was simply going to be a tough hike. Even their poster showed a green grass path up the mountain.

Well, it was much more than a tough hike. It was a technical climb.

We were required to have ice crampons fitted to our boots and needed ice picks and warm clothes so that when we got onto the glacier at the top you wouldn't get hypothermic. It was a difficult climb that none of us had trained for, and for most of us, it was also the first mountain we had ever attempted to climb.

To make matters even more difficult and complex, these 12 to 15 people did not know each other before we met in Doğubayazıt (the little village at the base of Ararat) and spent the first night before the climb together in a hotel. One of my friends and I were the only people that actually knew each other. He and I were comfortable with climbing and had prepared physically and mentally for months. We also roomed together to prepare for the climb together as well.

Interestingly though, right from the beginning, the morning we were to begin our climb, we found out that there were going to be a lot of other challenges, risks, and vulnerabilities as well. For instance, I was not found on the government's approved list to climb, so now my friend was worried and thought he would have to climb without me.

Eventually, I was found on the list and was able to climb with the rest of the team. But little things like that, just like things in life, sometimes keep us from staying positive in our thinking or from being able to reach our goal or goals because there are these little hurdles that just seem to pop out of nowhere at the most inopportune times. These unexpected obstacles, if you will, get in our way and can keep us from being able to smoothly reach our goal.

When we got to the base of Ararat, and we started our climb, we had no idea what to expect. No one really gave us any training, strategy, or understanding of what it was going to be like to climb. And yet, we spent the next three days climbing to the peak and back down again. Two people almost died. One due to altitude sickness, and the other due to hypothermia. We also learned the next day that 21 terrorists were on the mountain, which explained why there were so many military and police people with us. The jandarma and commandos were among us. But again, we didn't really know that until we had gotten up to the first camp and then realized that we had some terrorists on the mountain.

Some team members were worried and scared, and we all had a lot of sketchy thoughts where we might have come back and said, "You know, I don't think this is a good idea."

Or started to ask questions, like *Should I go or not go?*

Many people on the team were still wondering whether they were going to climb. At least we had those thoughts until we were dropped off at the base of the mountain, and there was no place to go but up. The decision time was now "go time."

In life, you may not have a 17,000-foot mountain physically in front of you. But you might have something else that seems like 17,000 feet that is keeping you from being able to reach your goals. When we're talking about coach-ability in this book, we explore the ability to coach yourself, even if you have internal fears or self-talk that is holding you back. Many times in life, we all experience having second thoughts, or we question the direction we are going in life and wonder whether our decisions were right or wrong, good or bad. Those kinds of things always come at us. The first person we have to be able to coach is ourselves.

When we reached the base of the mountain and started climbing up, it was nice and sunny, and there was no bad weather in sight. It wasn't really hot or anything like that either. The climb seemed to be going very well. At the first base camp, we settled in and spent a day acclimatizing. The next day we took off for the second camp.

By the third day, things began to change, and people started to feel the effects of altitude and the weather. Breathing at higher altitudes started to become difficult. Each breath now became a conscious labored breath, and each step felt like a huge goal in and of itself. I stayed behind with one of the women (I will call her Lee) who just wasn't feeling well, or at least at that time, she said she simply didn't feel well. Lee said she just felt tired. The rest of the team went on ahead.

I was by myself with Lee, so we took our time climbing. She had to sit down quite frequently to take rest breaks and it was pretty clear she was not doing well. I didn't know really what to think about what was happening and thought we likely just needed to rest because we were tired, right? Many of the team members had not done any exercise or physical training for this climb, so I just chalked up being tired as a result of being unprepared physically.

Unfortunately, I did not know anything about altitude sickness, which is what we later learned she was experiencing. The whole time I was thinking, What am I going to do if we have a bigger problem here? What if she passes out? That was my self-talk, and I had to keep coaching myself to say, Dane, it'll be fine. We're gonna make it through this. Later I had to do the same thing when it came to coaching the other teammates on our last leg of the climb to the peak. I would tell Lee, "You are doing real good. You're gonna be fine. We're gonna make it through this all the way to the second camp."

And we did. We successfully climbed to the second camp, which was around 15,000 feet. We were supposed to actually spend the night there, then wake up early in the morning at about 3:00 a.m. to start our final ascent to the peak. The goal was to make it to the peak and get off the glacier before noon when the sun would be melting the glacier and the ice under our feet would start to move and shift, which would be dangerous and give us even more things to worry about.

Once Lee and I reached the second camp, she wanted to go lie down in her tent because she was pretty tired. I was pretty tired too, but my adrenaline rush was not going to allow me to sleep, and I decided to just rest on the rocks in the sun.

Dane resting on rocks at 2nd Camp

About an hour later as the sun was going down, we realized that Lee was not just resting, she was actually going in and out of a coma, and her body was blowing up like a balloon from altitude sickness. In altitude sickness, the blood goes out to your extremities and doesn't return. We needed to make a life-and-death decision for Lee right away.

All of these people who never knew each other before this climb now had to huddle together and figure out what we were going to do for this teammate. We decided that even though it was at the end of the day with darkness coming on, the temperatures dropping, and 21 terrorists on the mountain, we were going to have to actually get her down off the mountain to save her life. That was the only way.

My friend Danny, another teammate, Greta (not her real name), and one of the climbing guides, Ahmet, decided to take Lee down the mountain in the dark. While Lee was in a coma, we tied Lee onto a donkey with a horsehair rope. Danny, Greta, and Ahmet led her down the mountain. That meant that Danny and Greta had to give up their goal and dream of climbing to the peak in order to save Lee's life. In our huddle, they had done just that. They made the decision to give up their goal of making it to the peak and sacrifice their ultimate, once-in-a-lifetime dream to save the life of another teammate. That was the toughest decision those teammates had to make at the time.

They were not worried any longer about whether they were going to make it to the top. In the blink of an eye, their goals had changed from personal needs and desires to the needs of someone else. They had become servant leaders.

To save Lee's life, the team had to be able to get her to a lower altitude because there wasn't really a solution for altitude sickness. She needed to return to a lower altitude so that she could readjust and return to normal. Fortunately this is just what they did. Once Danny left with Lee, I was by myself. My mind did mental gymnastics. Then I was starting to really question whether this climb was a good idea or not. I was also wondering if I was going to be okay myself. I didn't really know these other people and teammates. What if one of them put me in jeopardy? What if the terrorists attacked? What else might happen?

All that self-talk forced me to remind and coach myself that everything was going to be fine and that I would make it to the peak and back safely too. What a battle there was going on in my mind between emotions like fear and logic. Because of grit and self-coaching, I won the battle and eventually consoled myself by focusing on the goal of reaching the peak.

That night we went to sleep in our tents knowing morning would come very quickly. We started our ascent to the peak at about 2:30 a.m. that next morning. Some French and Italian teams had already come through our camp on their way to the peak before we had even gotten out of our sleeping bags.

When the next day began, we climbed up the rocky cliffs, using headlamps to light our way until daybreak and doing our best to find our way to the edge of the glacier. At this point, we definitely knew this climb was more than a tough hike. In the early morning with the bone-chilling cold and darkness, we climbed over rocks by feeling our way forward, inching our way up to the glacier area. In the process, I could tell several team members were having problems with their hearts. Their faces were bright red. Remember that many of them did not even train for this climb. Some of the team even mentioned that their hearts were racing, and they needed to sit down and rest more frequently. Now that we were on this technical climb at over 15,000 feet, breathing became labored as we climbed higher and higher. Oxygen in the air was very thin, and people's minds started to play games with them. Some even experienced minor hallucinations.

So, all of a sudden, I was not just trying to stay warm and safe myself, but I was coaching people in front of me, and coaching people behind me to keep going. It was quite a challenging adventure. Later, one of the team members who was climbing in front of me recalled that he kept passing out and said I would catch him enough to wake him back up and allow him to keep going. Fortunately, I just thought he was stumbling and did my best to help him keep going. I have no idea what I would have done had I known he was actually losing consciousness.

The point of this story is that in life, like on this climb, you never know at what point you need to coach yourself, prepare yourself, and be ready to coach others. It was a tough and extremely challenging climb. Without ice crampons or ice picks, we successfully arrived at the edge of the glacier. It was now time to put on our crampons, eat some good old raisins and peanuts (gorp), and get mentally ready for the final ascent.

Our guide (to the right in white coat) and one of our team members reaching the glacier's edge.

When we reached the edge of the glacier, another teammate, Maria (not her real name) sat down to rest in front of where I was sitting, and she immediately fell backward and went into convulsions. None of us knew what to do. We had a doctor with us, but when he came over to evaluate the condition of our teammate, he simply walked away. Someone needed to come up with a solution, but no one seemed to know what to do or had the energy to care. Therefore, I made the decision and took the lead to try to help. I wrapped my space blanket around Maria, put wool socks on her arms, and gave her an extra hat. All she had been wearing since we started climbing that morning was a thin windbreaker.

Eventually, the convulsions stopped, and with the space blanket wrapped around her body, she warmed up a little but was not consciously awake. She was looking around but was nonverbal, and we had no idea if she could walk or not. There was no help we could call for that would come and rescue us. Medical assistance was literally days away. The reality of the situation made me realize that it was up to us to save her, or she would just lie there and die. When I realized that she was actually awake and could respond to commands but couldn't speak, I put her crampons on her boots then got her up and ready to walk.

Now, I had another problem to deal with. The edge of the glacier had an ice sheet that was at a 60-degree slant and very dangerous. If I slipped or she slipped and we started to slide, it was over for us. There was nothing below to stop us except for a cliff, which we were sure to slide off and fall to our deaths. We are all supposed to be roped together and using our ice picks at this point in the climb.

Instead, I had to get her moving. In my haste, I did not get us roped in. I knew that despite the other threats and risks, her life was more important. I was able to get her up and walking, and with one of my hands holding the wrapped space blanket around her as I guided her, I took both ice picks in my other hand and coached her. We walked up the 60-degree incline of that glacier for quite a way. She was still nonverbal but was responding to my commands to start, stop, or lean on me for balance. In hopes of moving closer to the peak and getting warmed up, I had to keep her walking. As we later learned, this person was not only hypothermic but was experiencing altitude sickness and, thus, a comatose body.

The team set out on the glacier without the guide (in the white coat) leading the team and no one roped together.

Eventually, much later than planned, we made it to the peak just after noontime and even took pictures for the short time we were there. To this day, I don't think Maria remembers any of the climb to the peak. I even took a picture of her at the peak with Russia behind her. We had successfully made it to the top of Mt. Ararat.

The Team successfully on Top of Ararat at the Peak, 17,000ft.

Now the trick (in gymnastics terms) was to get all of us, including her, back down safely. Most people do not know that, in reality, the most dangerous part of a mountain climb is not necessarily the climb up. When climbers are going up a mountain, they keep their goal in mind and stay focused. Their adrenaline is pumping, and they are not completely exhausted. However, after the summit, when their adrenaline is gone and they are exhausted, they let their guard down. The focus they had going up is gone, and mentally, they become lazy. That is when real life-and-death troubles often occur.

Imagine that as we were descending, when we had to go back across the 60-degree glacier slant area, we had to focus as much as when we ascended—maybe even more. It would have been easy to rush each step and think the danger was over. But the danger was still real and present. We had to stay focused, and I had to carefully manage my teammate, who was, at that time, still responding to my coaching and commands but nonverbal and not fully conscious.

> *Our self-coaching and coaching by others are important in life, whether it is school, sports, family, or business. We have to stay focused with good self-talk and coaching.*

Sometimes, it's important to find humor when dangerous circumstances or things happen to surround us. As we were coming down from the peak, Maria was still comatose to a certain extent and nonverbal. She was walking in her sleep but able to respond to my commands. I coached her down from the 17,000-foot level to the second camp at around 15,000 feet.

It wasn't until we were about 200 yards from the second camp that she uttered her first words: "What are these doing on my arms?" she asked.

Remember, I had put a pair of my Turkish wool socks on her arms. Then I told her, "Those are my wool socks."

She took them off and gave them back to me. A few more steps and she asked, "Whose hat am I wearing?"

I had put my Snoopy hat on her head to keep her head warm. I was originally from northern Minnesota, and we were always taught that a large percentage of your body heat escapes through your head. I told her, "That's my hat."

She kind of just shrugged her shoulders, gave me my hat back, and kept walking. When we were about 20 yards from the tent, I told her that when she was back in her tent that she needed to take off my underwear and give it back to me as well. She looked quizzically at me, since by now she was fully awake and couldn't remember the climb at all. At that point, she was not sure if she had my underwear on or not. Then I told her I was just teasing her.

Finally, back at our tents, it was "mission accomplished." We had climbed to the peak and come back down from the glacier to safety and were now excited that we had been to the peak and were ready to tell our story to the other teammates who had sacrificed their opportunity to climb in order to save Lee's life.

Sometimes, we might not know when others need to coach us or who is able to coach us when we need help. Sometimes, we may not even recognize or realize that we need help. We may also find that help might come from the least expected place or the weakest person. We just never know. We may not even know or acknowledge that we do indeed need assistance or coaching. We simply have to stay coach-able.

There will also be times when you will need to coach others just to make it to the goal that maybe they set that wasn't your goal at all but was their goal to reach, and you had the wherewithal to help get them there. Just like my friends, teammates, and guides who had to sacrifice their personal goals to reach the top to allow Lee to live.

We've all seen these athletic races where someone's in the lead and they fall, and the person in second or third place picks that person up and helps run them across the finish line. And we call that great sportsmanship.

What those athletes did was a direct result of their character skills. They did not even have to think about it for very long. They just did the right thing at the right time for the right reason.

Just like Danny, Greta, and Ahmet, who didn't even see it as a sacrifice—they just did what they needed to do for Lee. Even I had chosen to stay behind with Lee when she started feeling ill because she needed me, and my character was not going to leave my teammate by herself. No one was left behind.

It is our character and character skills that really drive the people skills and technical skills, but it is the courage of the person in the seat of the tricycle who has to make the right decision at the right time and for the right reason. It takes courage, and sometimes there has to be some grit mixed in with that courage. That is where "heart math" kicks in, and it all starts to add up. (Note: we will explore heart math a little later in the book, and it will be an exciting topic to learn if you have never heard of it before.)

The character skills wheel on the Tricycle Effect allows us to grow and balance the back two wheels, as well as support and lead our team, families, and company or organizations with the front wheel, the character skills wheel, to lead with character first.

The competence wheel included technical skills like knowing how to use our ice crampons and ice picks and making that technical climb, which none of us were really trained for. The other competence wheel involved people skills, such as how well we looked out for others, thought of others before ourselves, and sacrificed for someone else with teamwork, communication, critical thinking skills, and problem-solving.

This story emphasized being coach-able and demonstrated how coach-ability happened in all three phases of that triad: coaching myself, coaching others, and having others coach me. The guide remained with us on the climb but hadn't told us what we were going to do to get to the peak at the beginning, but he still had to train us to wear our ice crampons and picks. If I had not been coach-able by others, if I had not been able to coach others, and if I had not coached myself, we would not have necessarily successfully saved Maria, who actually had hypothermia, or the team may not have saved Lee with altitude sickness. We might have lost someone due to those circumstances or some other circumstances that could have snowballed quickly into an emergency. Less importantly, we may not have completed the climb at all.

Instead, we all stuck together as a team. We made decisions in our huddles together. We worked together as a team, sacrificed together, and we made it to our collective goal: to get to the peak. We got all the way back down to the base of Ararat again and reunited with our teammates. We found that Lee, who had altitude sickness and whom we had to strap to the back of a donkey, had now recovered from the altitude sickness and was doing fine. Maria, the person I had helped with hypothermia on the glacier, was no longer comatose and was capable of talking with people as she had recovered and was on her way back to being healthy as well.

Remember that coach-ability has that coaching triad. It's very important that we stay coach-able in each of the legs of that coaching triad because we need to be prepared for ourselves and, more importantly, to be ready to assist with the needs and goals of others as well. Who knows when or if we will be called on to lead with character first and save the day.

All right, team, trike on!

3. Overview of the Coach-Ability Book

I hope you enjoyed the story of our climb up historic Mt. Ararat. This book explores the various aspects of coach-ability, with the triad of coach-ability of course, but it also includes more:

- The signs of coach-ability
- The benefits of coach-ability
- How to develop coach-ability
- Barriers to coach-ability
- How to overcome barriers to coach-ability
- How to encourage coach-ability in others
- Coach-ability in leadership and personal life

As you just experienced with the Mt. Ararat climb, throughout this book, you will have a better understanding of coach-ability and how to develop this essential trait for your personal and professional leadership growth.

Chalk Talk Coaching Tip

Coach-ability is about being open to feedback and learning from every experience to grow personally and professionally, just as a mountain climber must adapt and respond to unexpected challenges. It involves a triad of self-coaching, coaching others, and being open to coaching by others, all crucial for navigating the metaphorical mountains we face in life.

- **Promise of solution**: By embracing coach-ability, you commit to a journey of continual learning and adaptation, fostering personal and professional growth through a receptive and proactive mindset.

- **Suggested action step**: Start a feedback journal where you record and reflect on feedback received weekly. Make an actionable plan based on this feedback to address areas for improvement. This habit of reflection and action can bolster your coach-ability and contribute to your ongoing development.

Workbook for Coach-Ability, Chapter 3
The Definition of Coach-Ability

Fill-in-the-Blanks

1. Coach-ability is the ability to be open to _____, learn from experiences, and make positive changes to achieve personal and professional growth.

2. Being coach-able means having a growth mindset in all three ways of the coach-ability triad: _____, others, and by others.

3. Coach-ability is important because it helps us _____ to new challenges and improve our outcomes and success.

Reflective Questions

1. Can you recall a recent situation where being open to feedback helped you grow? How did it feel, and what did you learn from that experience?

2. Reflect on a time when you had to adapt quickly to an unexpected challenge. How did coach-ability play a role in how you handled it?

3. How does the story of climbing Mt. Ararat relate to facing challenges in your own life? Identify a "mountain" you are currently facing and how you can apply the principles of coach-ability to overcome it.

Summary of Chapter 3 Workbook

In this chapter, we learned that coach-ability involves the willingness to accept feedback, learn from various experiences, and embrace positive change for both personal and professional development. It encompasses a threefold approach: coaching yourself, coaching others, and being receptive to coaching from others. Being coach-able allows for identification and improvement in areas of our lives that can lead to better outcomes and successes. By understanding and practicing coach-ability, as illustrated through the challenging Mt. Ararat climb, we can overcome the mountains in our lives, turning obstacles into opportunities for growth and achievement.

Chapter 4
Signs of Coach-Ability

My best skill was that I was coachable. I was like a sponge, and aggressive to learn. — Michael Jordan[11]

Being coach-able is not just about being open to feedback and willing to learn. It is a combination of different traits that make up the overall attitude and behavior of a coach-able person as well as character skills such as humility, vulnerability, and loyalty. In this chapter, we will discuss the signs of coach-ability and what they mean.

As we discussed in the last chapter, coach-ability is the ability to be open to feedback, learn from experiences, and make positive changes to achieve personal and professional growth. Signs of coach-ability include active listening, willingness to learn and try new things, open-mindedness, self-awareness, responsibility, and accountability for actions.

> Challenge/Problem statement: While many people are open to feedback and learning, they often lack the composite character traits like humility, vulnerability, and loyalty that constitute true coach-ability.

Coach John Wooden is credited with saying, "A good coach can change a game. A great coach can change a life." I believe that wholeheartedly, and I also believe that coach-ability, our ability to be *coach-able* is the *key* to a more successful and significant life!

At the time of this writing, I am coming off two speaking engagements I did in which I focused on presentations around leading with character first as the most important method of being successful and significant in life by focusing on adding value to others. Eben Pagan says in his e-book *The Client-Getting Script: 11 Proven Words to Turn a Conversation Into a High-Paying Client*, "Coaches who are great at getting clients are excellent at one thing: Hearing when other people have needs and then following up on those needs with a coaching session to help them solve or get the needs met. Empaths (people who are good at sensing the emotions of others and the needs of others) are good at noticing when others have needs."[12]

It turns out that every conversation I had with people in the audience and at my conference booth just happened to always lead back to character skills with words like empathy, caring, and loyalty. I am an empath by my character. In other words, I am someone who senses automatically the needs in other people's lives.

After retiring from a university where I taught cybertechnology ethics, I realized that the answers to questions I asked students at the beginning of each semester about character, the instructor, and learning were very telling:

1. What is something you feel your instructor could do to help you succeed in this course? The most common answer was "be caring."

2. How can I best help you succeed? The most common answer was "empathy."

3. I asked them, "Should you be *loyal*, at face value, to an employer that hires you?" The most common answer was an immediate no from over 99% of the students. When asked why they did not consider loyalty required at face value, even if the employer was paying them a great salary with benefits and more, they answered simply that "their loyalty needed to be earned by the employer."

Notice that care, empathy, and loyalty are all character skills. Of course, the people I had discussions at the conference with were generally business people, and many of them were from the health and medical industry. We had just come out of COVID-19 lockdowns and remote-only learning. Therefore, this should probably not be all that surprising. What was surprising was the number of conversations with people who came from medical clinics and hospitals who were really disappointed in their workplaces and lack of good moral and character-driven leadership. I would ask them, "Is empathy missing in your clinic or hospital?"

The immediate reaction (notice I said *reaction*) was to roll their eyes and let me know that there was hardly any empathy there anymore at all. Everything it seemed had been whittled down—it's just business. In other words, *profit over patient* or *profit and business over people*.

Of all the places that used to demonstrate empathy and caring the most, clinics and hospitals are now almost devoid of any such character skills. For many personnel, their medical workplaces have become a jungle of upheaval, toxic (as they have shared with me) environments, and a place to simply survive so that employees can keep their jobs and feed their families.

They now have "rental docs" and "rental nurses" who are only filling in and have not built a relationship with their patients at all. It is as if they are simply working on a cadaver void of feelings and emotions, dreams, and desires.

As I learned with my own family members over the last couple of years, your personal physician does *not* ever come to visit you if you are in a hospital stay. It is just a job. It is obvious that it is *not* their passion or purpose in life to make a difference for the patients. Of course, they simply need to meet their technical quota.

In essence, what I was hearing is that the medical field is filled with people who are focused on managing things to get results, and are not coach-able—at least in terms of management and leadership.

If they were coach-able, they would follow their heart and not their pocketbook. That way, trust could be developed in a deeper and more genuine way, and healing patients could be their most important focus and goal.

Those are just a couple of symptoms, but they are not the causes. Let's dig in a little deeper to the signs of coach-ability and see if we can learn some technical ways of connecting with people by using the character skills in The Tricycle Effect.

1. Active Listening

Active listening is a critical sign of coach-ability. Individuals who are coach-able are attentive and engaged listeners. They are open to hearing different perspectives and are willing to consider new ideas and perspectives. One of the most interesting things I have learned in the last year is this: the words *listen* and *silent* have exactly the same letters and number of letters in their words. Amazing! Did you know that? I didn't.

I do think it helps us understand how important being silent is to the genuine ability to listen.

Speaking of being silent to listen—can you listen with your heart? If you have empathy, you can definitely listen with your heart. When I say that, you could just blow that off, or you could listen to what I am about to share with you and take it to heart, literally.

First, why do we sometimes say or hear others say, "She/he speaks from the heart?"

Second, why does the Bible refer to our heart in many places? For instance, in Luke 6:45 the Bible says, "A good man brings good things out of the good stored up in his heart, and an evil man brings evil things out of the evil stored up in his heart. For the mouth speaks what the heart is full of."[13]

The heart has treasure! Who knew?!

Third, we learn from the book of Proverbs in the Bible that "above all else, guard your heart, for everything you do flows from it."[14]

Why do you think the Bible talks about the heart in the sense that it drives much of what we do and say? Interesting, isn't it?

It would be great if we could actually find a connection between our hearts and our minds.

Well, strangely enough, there is!

Have you ever heard of "heart math?" Yes, math, like mathematics. HeartMath is a company () that has developed practical solutions for relieving stress and anxiety, improving health and wellness, enhancing spirituality, and improving your performance. I have no affiliation with HeartMath whatsoever, but it is extremely interesting to study the work of HeartMath and to read stories of transplant recipients, including watching video testimonials about the phenomenon that allegedly connects the heart and the head together. Check it out further at: https://www.heartmath.com/

There are stories of heart transplant recipients who have experienced changes in their personalities, memories, behaviors, preferences, and habits from the donor whose heart they received.[15] Can you imagine one of the heart transplant recipients having some of the donor's memories that took place with experiences or events they have never had themselves?

Researchers are indeed discovering that our hearts and minds do have connections to each other.[16] Think about acupuncture or acupressure. We all know that certain places on or in the body map to other places in or on the body.

Well, we also now know that when you and I were embryos and just developing, as our bodies started to unfold and take the shape of the top of our body and the bottom of our body, some brain cells (neurons) remained in our hearts, and some heart cells remained in our brains. It is not hard to understand that without transplanting the brain, and only transplanting the heart, a heart transplant recipient may very well have some brain cells (neurons) and memories from the heart donor. Some researchers are even calling the area in our heart with brain cells the heart's "little brain."[17]

If that is the case, and the heart and mind are tied much closer together than we have realized in the past, what does that mean for us in terms of coach-ability? Well, for one thing, that means that in terms of listening, we can *actually* listen with the heart, just as the Bible tells us we have treasure in our hearts and can listen and speak from the abundance of our hearts. Listening with the heart is another way to describe the character skill related to empathy.

You see, we really are more complex human becomings than we may rightly know. Check it out further, at. They actually have a whole system, including technology devices with a smartphone app to help you connect your brain to your heart and learn real-time heart rhythm coherence, biofeedback, and evidence-based techniques to live a healthier, happier life. Again, I have no affiliation with HeartMath, other than using their smartphone app to help me become more heart-mind smart.

With that in mind, be careful what you think about and what you say so that your heart is filled with character-istics and values that will reflect a coach-able you.

2. Willingness to Learn and Try New Things

Individuals who are coach-able are open to learning and trying new things. They are not afraid to take risks and step outside of their comfort zone. They embrace opportunities to develop new skills and strategies and are committed to personal and professional growth.

This also means they are not afraid to fail and even fail often.

This is one of the most difficult challenges in the gym for our athletes to believe and then learn. Let me explain.

I was standing at our gymnastics uneven bars one night while coaching gymnasts, and one of the newer gymnasts who had just joined stepped up to take a turn. I had not met this new gymnast yet, and we were working on a simple little skill like gliding under the bars. So I told her to go ahead and start, but she didn't go.

I told her again that she could go, and no response. She was just staring ahead with no expression on her face, like she was in a trance.

So I asked her, "Why aren't you going?"

She said, "Because I am afraid that I might fail."

Immediately, I thought to myself, Fail at what? We are just doing a little glide here, and there is nothing to fail at all.

But to her, it was a big deal, and she was scared that she might fail. I had to really think about that for a moment, and even then I was struggling to understand why she might be afraid to fail.

So I asked point-blank, "Why are you afraid to fail?"

To me, as a coach and teacher, her response was shocking. She very clearly and confidently said, "Because my teacher at school says failure is a bad thing, and anyone who tells you that you have failed is a bad person." I could not imagine the pressure this little gymnast felt, knowing that if she failed, that would be a bad thing. This event had now turned into coaching a character skill moment.

I stopped practice, and we had a little discussion about three things:

1. "Failure is only the opportunity to more intelligently to begin again." — Henry Ford[18]

2. Failing forward and feeling free in failure is important in any learning process. Ryan Leak says, "You'll achieve a lot more by chasing failure rather than chasing success."[19]

3. "Failure is an event and not a person." — Zig Ziglar[20]

I explained and coached this little athlete on the fact that she was going to fail in our gym—a lot. And we celebrate it because each failure brings us closer to learning a skill or doing a successful routine. Today, she is still in our gym and a very successful athlete who now understands that failure is simply a stepping-stone to success.

Have you ever thought about what you do when you start to walk? What is the first thing you do? A lot of people will say things, like *Think about it*, *Take a first step*, or *Make a decision*. There are lots of things people might say, but there is only one thing that will keep you from starting to walk, and if you don't do that thing, you will not be able to walk normally. Why is that?

You have to fall!

You have to fall forward to walk. In reality, that means we are all walking around in a controlled fall.

This also explains why older people fall to the ground more and are hurt more often as they age. They try to walk, but their feet and legs do not get out in front of them fast enough, so they just fall down.

Well, I tell my little athletes they should feel *free* to fail. Just like they are free to fall in walking to move ahead in life, they must be free to fail in doing anything in life, especially when learning gymnastics. It is also fun to be free to fail forward in our journey of learning in life.

Remember that I told you that we are really just big kids now that we are all grown up? Well, we need to go back and bring forward some of those lessons we knew when we were children and adopt them as adults. If we had been afraid to fail, we would never have learned to walk. Thank goodness none of us counted or kept track of the number of times we fell while learning to walk, and thankfully, most of us don't remember many of those successful failures growing up.

So we just feel free to fail in order to be willing to try, make an effort, and learn new things. We teach the athletes and students in our gym that *trying is not good enough*. Many of our athletes come to us believing that trying *is* good enough. For those of us in business and sports, we know that you don't get much for simply trying. So, we replace the word *trying* with *effort*. Trying is not good enough in life—we must actually do it. The effort is very important, but won't necessarily get us to our goal(s). I simply expect each of my athletes to fail forward and have fun in making the effort to learn and to fail forward successfully.

3. Open-Mindedness

Open-mindedness is another critical sign of coach-ability. Coach-able individuals are open to new ideas and perspectives, not closed off to alternative viewpoints. They are willing to consider different ways of thinking and doing things.

There are times when each of us use common language while we self-talk or coach ourselves. Those words have the power to build up or break down. Let me give you an example with a three-letter word: *yet*. I call this lesson the power of yet.

If I had a nickel for each time, over the last 30-some years, when I heard someone say, "I can't do that," or "I won't do that," I would be rich. As we just discussed with the action of trying being replaced with effort, there is a way to make these sentences build us up and not break us down or hold us back from successfully accomplishing our task or goal. There is a simple way to do that.

What if you just replace *I can't do that*, which is a sentence that conveys no progress is possible, with *I can't do that* yet!

If you say each of those two sentences to yourself, you will find that each sentence elicits a different feeling inside you. Pay attention to how you feel when you say them and really mean them. Try it! When you say, "I can't do that," you give yourself no opportunity to even make an effort (i.e., try) again.

But, when you say, "I can't do that *yet*," now you are saying, "I will eventually do it, and I am free to fail and make another effort." See the difference between those two sentences. You can even feel the difference. That is the difference that self-talk can make in allowing us to fail forward in life.

If I hear a gymnast say, "I can't do that," then I know they are closed minded and most likely will not even make a good effort. They are probably not coach-able either. It is then that I tell them, "I am not an English teacher, but I do know that you need to finish your English sentences."

The first time I tell them that, they look at me quizzically. I say it again. Then if they haven't gotten it (and sometimes the more veteran gymnasts are giggling because they have most likely heard the same lesson themselves), I tell the gymnasts they need to finish their sentences with *yet*.

"*I can't do that yet!*"

It is almost like cutting off the apostrophe and the letter *T*.

That one word *yet* makes all the difference in the world.

The power of yet keeps us open-minded so we can stay coach-able.

4. Self-Awareness

Self-awareness is an essential sign of coach-ability. Individuals who are coach-able have a clear understanding of their strengths and weaknesses. They are open to feedback and constructive criticism and willing to make positive changes to improve their performance.

Coach-ability starts with self-coaching, and that starts with self-talk, whether by words, images, feelings, or emotions.

A great example of this is when our athletes are working out on the balance beam in gymnastics practices. Many coaches will tell a gymnast something like *Don't bobble* or *Don't fall*. Well, we have learned over the years that people think more about whatever someone tells us *not* to think about. Likewise, we will most likely do whatever someone says when they warn us, "Don't do _____" (fill in the blank).

I think we are just structured like that. If someone tells us not to, we are going to do that very thing, consciously or unconsciously.

Instead, if we understand that concept of coaching, we will be kinder to ourselves and to others if we coach them with something like *Focus on the end of the beam when you are finishing your full turn*, instead of *Don't bobble at the end of your full turn*.

We did not give them a way to finish their full turn without a bobble if we simply command them with the word *don't*. But we communicate the solution—and keep them from automatically thinking about falling or bobbling—if we give them a positive action to move toward, focus on, and make a change with.

Being self-aware then entails both sides of coaching. The coach must understand motivation when it comes to human becomings and must also understand the natural "bent" or response from them as well and must apply it to self-coaching even while coaching others.

Some of my very best coaches with the best ideas are still preschoolers who do the darndest things when you ask or coach them. I have even learned some of the best lead-ups for drills to help my most advanced athletes with their skills.

5. Responsibility and Accountability for Actions

I like to tell people, "I am a teacher by degree and a coach by profession." In other words, I am not only a school teacher and gymnastics coach, but I am also an IT professional. I have been in IT for over 40 years. I got my start in IT in the U.S. Air Force over 30 years ago, where we were already developing very advanced technologies that have only come about in the public sector here in the United States in the last five to 10 years.

In the United States, we like to think we are far ahead technologically compared to the rest of the world. I have news for you. We are actually very far behind in many respects. I think the reason we believe we are the furthest ahead is that we don't see anyone in front of us any longer. As it turns out, that might be a result of other countries being so far ahead of us that we just simply no longer see them in front of us. They have gone over the horizon and are out of sight.

Let me give you an example. In 1987, my boss (our group commander and President Reagan's communications director in the White House) and I were actually using Zenith Z-100 laptops (Zenith used to make laptops) across Motorola's first mobile phones. And guess where we were? Of all places in the world, we were stationed in Ankara, Turkey. That is right, we were all wireless in Turkey in the 1980s. Here in the United States, we did not actually have that capability for almost two decades after that.

Because I have been in IT for so long, I have watched some of the very newest technology be born and evolve over four decades. It has been exciting and powerful. However, I have also learned that every technology, bar none, can be used for good or bad purposes.

With that in mind, every technology created, designed, and used, comes with a responsibility to use it for safe and healthy purposes rather than to abuse or use it for evil and even deadly purposes.

Responsibility is a character skill, and even though IT technology involves the technical skill wheel of the Tricycle Effect, it also most certainly involves the people skill wheel. This is especially true as it relates to how technology affects and influences others, for good or bad, and the character skills of responsibility and accountability.

With the responsibility character skill, there must be a way to hold people responsible for their actions and the results of their actions. That is called accountability. So, accountability is also a character skill.

Let me give you an example of this in reference to the technology we all use: smartphones, social media, and now artificial intelligence.

Most of the time, students came into my class thinking they knew a lot about technology only to find out about halfway through the semester that they were not the customer as they had thought, but that they were the product being sold, in terms of their privacy and intellectual property.

The students generally thought that because we had *ethics* in the class title, we would be studying some type of philosophical ethics. They learned that there actually is something called character ethics. Character ethics is not so much about philosophy as it is about practicing ethics in our everyday lives. And it's not just students who don't grasp the idea at first. I've met many PhDs who have no idea what character ethics really are.

Practical character ethics, as in the Tricycle Effect, is simply the study of right and wrong involving character skills like responsibility and accountability.

A few years ago, I was chosen from over 120 people in over 20 countries to present a concept in cybertechnology ethics, which I call the Houdini concept, at an ethics conference on the East Coast. Remember Harry Houdini, the great magician and escape artist? He seemingly believed there was not a lock in the world that could not be broken into or out of.

To explain the Houdini concept a little more, let me introduce a concept that many of us in IT fields call the human factor. In the IT field, it is known that the weakest link in internet security or cybersecurity is the human. Yes, that is correct. You and I are the weakest link when it comes to internet security. In addition, Harry Houdini believed that if something was built by a human, it could be broken into by a human as well. So, if we put the human factor together with the fact that if humans built it, then humans can break into it, you have the Houdini concept in a nutshell.

Just like Harry and locks, humans and internet security are parallel concepts, which result in the understanding that if a hacker wants to breach a target, they will simply use a human to do that, versus trying to break through firewalls, antivirus tools, or whatever other protection we may have put in place to keep the bad guys out. Think of it like this. We have to cover up all the holes that a hacker might use to get into our network or computer, but the hacker or bad guy only needs to find one hole. That makes humans the weakest link since they only need to make one careless mistake, and the bad guys are in. I will have more to say on this whole concept, along with cyber and internet security, in my next book, titled *Artificial Intelligence Unveiled and The Tricycle Effect*.

After being chosen to speak at the ethics conference, I traveled to Old Dominion University in Virginia to give the Houdini concept presentation to dozens of PhDs. I received very little feedback from any of them afterward, so I inherently thought I had done poorly and failed at communicating my Houdini concept message on cybersecurity and character ethics.

However, at lunch, I found out that some people at my table said they really enjoyed my presentation, but they wanted to know what the strange term they had never heard was.

I didn't understand the question, so I asked, "What strange term did I use?"

I could not imagine any terms I used as being strange, let alone unknown to PhDs. They answered, "Character ethics."

I'd used the term *character ethics* but had not defined it for the audience, so they were wondering what character ethics was the whole time.

I thought character ethics was self-evident but learned that it was not, evidently, at least to some of these PhDs. So, I failed in one area and learned to define character ethics better from then on for all of my audiences.

It seems that today, we not only cannot define character ethics, but we no longer really know what character ethics and character skills are or look like in action. I call the practice of living out good character skills in life character in action or character in motion! We know it when we see it, but we can't articulate it very well, since it has been eradicated from our vernacular and common language these days and is not taught consistently in the homes with families or in most schools with teachers.

After over 40 years in IT and having run my own IT cybersecurity business for 30 years, I believe in the Houdini concept and the fact that the human factor is the weakest link when it comes to cybertechnology security. I have seen it firsthand and understand how most CEOs we worked for were not coach-able since they refused to believe that their company networks were hackable.

I also believe in the Houdini concept, with the human factor being the weakest link to cybertechnology and character ethics.

What is the weakest link when it comes to cybersecurity? The human factor!

What is the weakest link when it comes to character ethics? The human factor!

No matter how secure you make your technology with software like antivirus or antimalware, etc., and no matter how secure you make your technology with hardware like routers and firewalls, the bad guys will always hack or break in if they want to target you and get access to your network with the hardware and software. How? They just search for your company's weakest link, which is someone (employee, vendor, or customer) who will do something they should not have or will not do something they should have.

Nothing built by humans is 100% secure, and it never will be 100% secure!

It is also important to realize that with every technology comes a new level of responsibility based on the fact that the technology can be used for good or bad intentions and actions.

We don't often think about this, but it is true. We judge others by their actions, and we judge ourselves most often by our intentions. Intentions are not actions. Intentions are good, but it is the actions that set reality.

So how do we strengthen the human factor, both for technology and character ethics? By intentionally training for the character skills and growing the values that drive excellent leadership, engagement, and healthy cultures in our companies, schools, organizations, and families.

In addition, teamwork is also a key solution. Because with a team, you have accountability. Having a teammate makes you better than you can be all by yourself, whether it is in the realm of cybersecurity or character skills and ethics.

At a minimum, the most simple, basic and smallest team is made up of two people. That can mean marriage, where each mate holds the other in high honor and respect and holds them accountable. (At least that is how it should be. See chapter 18 in *The Tricycle Effect* for a discussion and teaching on the tradition of marriage and how that relates to character skills.)

To really bring home this concept of responsibility and accountability in being coach-able, we need to realize that every new technology that emerges also has a corresponding need for us as members of humanity to ensure we are responsible with it and use it wisely and safely.

There is a need to hold people and companies accountable for the technology they create or build. Many people are calling for accountability to be the solution to our AI train that is rolling down the tracks today at an ever-increasing rate of speed with no safety considerations or accountability. Accountability also hints at holding people accountable for their actions and behavior through discipline or punishment for those who do the wrong thing with technology and use it for ill or bad.

However, there is a flipside to accountability also where we reward and acknowledge those who do the right thing with technology and use it to further humanity, demonstrating good character skills: trustworthiness, kindness, respect, fairness, loyalty, empathy, etc.

Coach-able individuals take responsibility for their actions and are willing to be held accountable for their behavior. They recognize the impact of their actions on others and are committed to making positive changes in growing their character skills. Reading and learning about The Tricycle Effect can help to improve relationships and outcomes between humans.

In conclusion, coach-ability is an essential trait that can lead to personal and professional character- and values-driven leadership growth. Active listening, willingness to learn to try new things, open-mindedness, self-awareness, responsibility, and accountability for actions are critical signs of coach-ability.

By developing these signs of coach-ability, individuals can achieve their goals, unlock their full potential, and make a positive impact in their personal and professional lives. Adding growth and improvement in developing your character skills will help you *lead with character first* in everything you do and allow you to be successful in adding value to yourself and to others.

Trike on!

Chalk Talk Coaching Tip

Coach-ability encompasses traits like active listening, willingness to learn, and open-mindedness, all of which are key for personal and professional growth. It's not just about being open to feedback but also about taking responsibility, being self-aware, and staying accountable, which together shape a character that's poised for success and significance.

- **Promise of solution**: By understanding and cultivating the signs of coach-ability, individuals can strengthen their character and enhance their ability to grow personally and professionally.

- **Suggested action step**: Practice active listening in your daily interactions by summarizing what others say before responding. This will not only show that you value their input but also help you to develop empathy and open-mindedness, which are key aspects of coach-ability.

Workbook for Coach-Ability, Chapter 4

SIGNS OF COACH-ABILITY

Fill-in-the-Blanks

1. Coach-ability is not just about being open to feedback. It's about being willing to learn and possessing character skills like _____, _____, and loyalty.

2. Being coach-able involves traits such as active listening, willingness to learn to try new things, and _____.

3. The ability to be coach-able is the *key* to a more successful and _____ life.

Reflective Questions

1. Think of a time when active listening changed the outcome of a situation for you. What was the scenario and what did you learn from truly hearing the other person?

2. Reflecting on your personal experiences, can you identify a moment when being open to learning and trying new

things led to an unexpected success or breakthrough?

3. How do you balance the drive to be successful with the importance of being open-minded and coach-able in both your personal and professional life?

Summary of Chapter 4 Workbook

Chapter 4 delves into the various traits that constitute coach-ability, extending beyond just the capacity to accept feedback to encompass a more comprehensive set of character skills. This workbook encourages readers to identify and reflect on moments where these traits have played pivotal roles in their lives. By connecting these attributes to real-life scenarios, readers can gain a deeper understanding of how coach-ability influences both personal development and professional advancement. The chapter emphasizes the significance of humility, vulnerability, open-mindedness, self-awareness, and a sense of responsibility, all of which contribute to your ability to lead a more fulfilled and meaningful life. It asserts that a coach-able person is not only receptive to growth but also actively seeks out opportunities to improve and accepts accountability for their actions.

CHAPTER 5

The Benefits of Coach-Ability—Coach-Leader

Every day, I encourage others to add value to people. — John C. Maxwell[21]

BEING COACH-ABLE HAS NUMEROUS benefits that can positively affect all areas of your life. In this chapter, we will explore the benefits of being coach-able, including faster personal and professional values-driven leadership growth where character values drive solid leadership first, which then leads to improved relationships with others, higher job satisfaction and career success, improved leadership skills, and better mentoring abilities.

> Challenge/Problem statement: Personal and professional growth can often be hampered by a lack of openness to feedback and an unwillingness to embrace change and constructive criticism.

1. Faster Personal and Professional Growth

Coach-ability can lead to faster personal and professional growth. By being open to feedback and constructive criticism, individuals can identify areas for improvement and develop new skills and strategies. Without that feedback, growth will most likely be slower or may even be nonexistent. So, personal and professional growth cannot be done effectively by going it alone or by chance. Your personal and professional growth must be goal oriented and intentional by design. Coach-ability can help individuals develop a growth mindset, which can help them overcome obstacles and setbacks and achieve their goals more quickly as well. Without feedback, you will have a very difficult time achieving your dream goals. As Ken Blanchard said, "Feedback is the breakfast of champions."[22]

As we all journey through life, we get older and, hopefully, wiser. One of my mentors, John C. Maxwell, is no different. Even though he has written many books on leadership, he is still growing and learning about leadership. More importantly, I can tell you that he is still growing his character skills. The following is an excerpt from a presentation I did on living a life with character first, in which I highlighted how John believes that *character is the foundation of leadership.*

Thought Leaders and Their Twilight Years on Character

There are many other people out there, too, who are doing many different things to try to make a difference in their world. I've noticed that some of them, like Stephen Covey and Zig Ziglar, have started to focus on how important it is to have great character skills and how that correlates to effective leadership and a fulfilling life.

Zig Ziglar was one of the leaders who, at the end of his life, made character one of the main topics in his books, speeches, and presentations. So was Stephen Covey, especially in his book *The 7 Habits of Highly Effective People*.[23]

Both of them have passed away now, but John C. Maxwell is actually following in their footsteps and doing the same thing. In his most recent book, *High Road Leadership*, John focuses more finitely on character and what it means to do the right thing at the right time and for the right reason. I noticed this trend where people in their twilight years focus more on character for significance than on all these other things in management and leadership for success.

I believe that tells us a great deal about how important it is to build a great foundation of leadership with character. It's more about significance than success at that late stage of life. It should have been that way for each of us at every stage of life and even more so in the twilight years. Building that foundation of leadership based on character skills allows us to journey faster to personal and professional growth.

In John's original book, *Developing the Leader Within You*, John titled chapter 3 "Integrity." His subtitle was "The Most Important Ingredient in Leadership."[24]

Notice he simply says integrity is an ingredient. We never stop learning, and if we're a coach or a teacher who values growing as a leader, we love to keep coaching and teaching.

Now read what John did in version two of that same book when he updated it years later. He changed chapter 3's title to "Character: The Foundation of Leadership."

That was a direct result of his actual continued intentional growth in leadership. So, arguably, here is the world's top leadership expert, who's written well over 80 books on leadership, and he's still growing. That means you can too. You can continue to grow as a leader faster and stronger by seeking out feedback and being intentional, especially when you focus on character as your foundation of leadership.

Don't forget to lead with character first, team! Trike on!

2. Improved Relationships with Others

Coach-ability can also lead to improved relationships with others. By being open to feedback and constructive criticism, individuals can improve their ability to listen actively and communicate effectively. Coach-ability can help individuals seek out the perspectives and opinions of others, which can help build the character skills of trust and respect.

Mo Gawdat, a past Google X chief business officer, recommends that you "treat others as you would like to be treated. If you would fear that the way you're using AI is going to harm your daughter, don't harm anyone else by using it."[25] There is an abundance of opportunity in ethical businesses.

Mo continues by saying, "That is the essence of ethics. Treat others as you would like to be treated."[26]

That is called the Golden Rule. John C. Maxwell discusses this in his *Ethics 101* book. "I believe you will be able to use one guideline to govern all your ethical decision-making. It's based on the Golden Rule." John further says, "I believe the Golden Rule can become your North Star when it comes to ethical navigation."[27]

Furthermore, John quotes his mentor, Fred Smith Sr., as saying, "You know, a version of the Golden Rule exists in just about every culture."[28] Isn't that amazing?

I actually taught this in my university cybertechnology ethics classes for years, and among all the students I had from around the world, not once did any of them suggest or question that their culture did not have any such rule.

This is the rule I set for each of my students in every class I taught: *We will treat each other as we would like to be treated.* Especially when it came to their research paper topic, each student understood that we would respect the opinions of other students even if they conflicted with or contradicted our own beliefs or opinions, and we would respect the topic and position they chose as well.

That is the essence of the Golden Rule: "Do unto others as you would have them do unto you."

It worked great. Students felt safe and free to express themselves, and they had great public discourse while in class, where respect for each other was honored.

Based on that, I would like to suggest that there is a common language that pervades every culture and ties all of humanity together, and that is what the Golden Rule aims to accomplish: *Care* for each other as human becomings. If you acted more with care, you would become a "care actor." You would become a person who leads with character first in life.

3. Higher Job Satisfaction and Career Success

Coach-ability can also lead to higher job satisfaction and career success. By being open to feedback and constructive criticism, individuals can identify areas for improvement and develop new skills and strategies. Coach-ability can also help individuals adapt to changes and new challenges in the workplace, which can lead to career success.

Let me share a story with you that I also learned in one of my discussions with an owner/CEO of a new company. The company had just garnered a lot of venture capital. This owner/CEO and their administrative assistant were visiting with me at my booth during a conference, and I asked them how they were doing in their business. The owner said they were doing really well. I let them know that I was hearing just the opposite from other business owners.

I also shared that I had visited recently with nurses from different clinics and hospitals, and they all agreed that empathy in their workplaces was one of the most important things that was missing.

Once I shared that feedback, the owner told me that his business had experienced a really bad sales track record for quite some time while trying to get his new company off the ground. He went on to say that he eventually, and by accident, hired some nurses. Most of them quit their jobs in the medical workforce because of the toxic work environments and lack of good leadership. The nurses were so burned out and tired of being in the medical system that they left and went to look for another job outside the medical arena.

The owner told me that after he hired them, his sales started to skyrocket. In fact, he said he has never had such good sales. Imagine that—nurses as your salespeople.

He said that one of the most important sales skills he discovered was—you guessed it—empathy. Nurses are nurses because they care, and most of them are empaths too. He hires nurses now for all his salespeople and staff.

Great character and character skills are absolutely essential to success, but people want to feel significant as well. That means they want to find joy in life by adding value to others first. As a result, they find joy in the journey and become significant to others.

Hopefully, throughout this book, what I teach, coach, and share with you will inspire you to lead with character first in everything you do and remember that character skills and walking through life daily by putting the people (patients) before profits is the best return and investment any company can earn.

You can actually get a greater return on character just as you aim for a return on investment. By the way, research proves that as well.

It is hard to find the research, but comprehensive research has been done and continues to be done. A prime example of that research can be found in a book titled *Return on Character* by Fred

Kiel at the KRW Corporation. Fred asks a great question, "Does the character of our leaders matter?"[29] What do you think?

He answers that question in the subtitle of his book, "The Real Reason Leaders and Their Companies Win." Through Fred's research, we find that character does indeed matter, and that is the real reason leaders and their companies win. They focus on the character of their employees and, as a result, yield a higher return on their assets than other companies that do not.

Character Counts and Character Matters!

So, be careful if you are in the medical industry. If you don't take care of your nurses, they will go somewhere else to take care of someone else. Be kind and care…always.

Life can be challenging at times. It can be difficult to navigate through various obstacles and setbacks, especially when we feel stuck and unsure of how to move forward. That's where coach-ability comes in and why, just like my Mt. Ararat climb, we need teams of people around us who can make us better than we can be by ourselves—both in how we feel about life as well as in making better decisions in our journey. That is what makes life really rich as a human becoming, isn't it?

By being coach-able and open to feedback, learning from life's experiences, and making positive changes, individuals can achieve personal and professional growth, improve relationships, and fulfill their potential. You don't have to go it alone! You can be coach-able and team up with others in your life's journey! Trike on!

4. Improved Leadership Skills Lead to Improved Relationships

Coach-ability is an essential trait for effective leadership based on our influence with others. By being open to feedback and constructive criticism, leaders can identify areas for improvement and develop new skills and strategies, which include the ability to work more effectively and productively with other people. Coach-ability can also help leaders develop a growth mindset, which can help them overcome obstacles and setbacks and achieve their goals—both personally and within the cultures of their families and teams.

When leaders develop a growth mindset, it is natural for them to cast vision and embrace values, both for themselves and for their team, personally as well as professionally.

> *"Leaders stand for something—Vision. Leaders stand on something—Values."*— Dr. Myles Munroe[10]

Coach-able leaders who practice character skills tend to have better relationships with others, both personally and professionally. People gravitate to other people who care about them, respect them, trust them, and are fair. All of those actions are character skills that we must practice if we are to grow our network of friends, colleagues, and clients. Additionally, coach-able leaders are more open to feedback and suggestions, which can improve communication and collaboration with others. Being coach-able can also make individuals more approachable and easier to work with, which can lead to stronger and more positive relationships.

A perfect example of this is a story I shared in my first book, *The Tricycle Effect*. I want to reshare that story to illustrate how coach-ability with the power of character in the Tricycle Effect helped me build a very healthy and long-lasting relationship with Mikey, one of my students in a middle school I was substitute teaching at on a long-term basis.

(Excerpt from *The Tricycle Effect*)[31]

After serving my country as an officer in the United States Air Force, I returned home to Wisconsin and obtained a teaching job as a long-term substitute physical education teacher at a local school. I was excited to get back to teaching again. I had graduated from college with a bachelor's degree in physical education. Teaching and coaching were always my passions. The physical education teacher I was subbing for had to take an extended leave from teaching, and therefore, I had a great opportunity to be able to teach long-term without committing to a permanent job.

Getting to the school on my first day was very exciting. It was even more exciting that this was the first day of the new school year, so everyone was excited and ready for what the new year was going to bring. I remember walking into the school with everyone roaming the hallways and finding their classes. I was so grateful to be back in school again, especially with the opportunity to be a teacher again.

One thing happened, though, right at the beginning of the school day that really changed my outlook on that first day of school. In almost every single class that I had that morning in the elementary school, a different teacher would ask me if I had met

Mikey yet. Of course, I hadn't had Mikey yet, and as I found out later, he was a middle school student, and I didn't teach middle school until the afternoon.

As the morning wore on, and as more teachers asked me if I had met Mikey yet, it was obvious that Mikey was going to be a real challenge. When I told the teachers I had not had him yet, they just chuckled or laughed out loud. So as it turned out, my first morning of elementary school went very smoothly. That afternoon I went over to the middle school, ate lunch, and proceeded to my first class.

When the bell rang, I entered the gymnasium, expecting to see some kids politely waiting for me to arrive and start class. Instead, what I saw was like something out of the movie Animal House.

Kids were running around, some of them had climbed up into the bleachers, some had their butts in the basketball hoops—mostly it was just pure chaos. As I walked closer to the middle of the gym, I asked one of the students who seemed to be somewhat quiet, or at least quieter, if he knew who Mikey was. At that point in time, all the students started laughing.

Again, I asked where Mikey was, and all of a sudden, a young man from the back of the group walked forward, and other kids who were in the group in the middle backed away as he walked through the middle of the group up to the front where I was standing.

This young man said, "I'm Mikey. What do you want?"

I said, "Well, Mike, I'm Coach D, and I want you to be the leader in warming up the class today."

Mikey's tone of voice immediately changed, and he said, "I can't lead—I don't know how."

I asked him why, and Mikey said, "Because I've never led anything before."

And I said, "Doesn't matter. I will help you and teach you how to lead. I'll be right here with you."

So Mikey and I started our calisthenics and warm-up routine for the class. From that point on, Mikey never acted up, nor did he encourage any of the other kids in class to act up either. The other kids in class just seemed to follow him and respect him in a very natural way.

For two weeks, Mikey helped me lead the class and helped provide a teaching environment and structure for what was, most likely, the best physical education classes most of those kids had experienced in a very long time.

However, my long-term subbing was about to end prematurely. The teacher I was subbing for was coming back a lot earlier than originally anticipated.

At the end of the two weeks, on my last day, I was in my office in the locker room, finishing up paperwork and finalizing the grade book, when all of a sudden, I could hear the door to my office close.

I looked up, and I saw Mikey with his back to me as he was closing the door. And as he turned around, I could see huge tears flowing down his cheeks.

I said, "Mikey, what's the matter?"

And Mikey's reply to me was profound.

Mikey said, "Mr. D, what will I do now that you're leaving? You're the only teacher that ever cared about me."

This was the Mikey who all the teachers had warned me about?

He transformed into a responsible and respectful young man. Unlike the other teachers, I saw Mikey as I believed he could be, not what he was living up to just because the teachers had him marked or labeled that way.

With a little hesitation and concern in my voice as well, I told Mikey that he would do just fine without me. He just needed to be the leader that he was capable of being. I told him I hoped that I had given him the ability to see himself as what he could be and not what other teachers thought he was or should be.

I don't know where Mikey is today, but I hope that the life experience with me by his side, for that short period of time in life, helped pave the way to make him a strong leader: a leader who cared about others and could help mold their lives into what they could be and not what others thought them to be as well.

So what was it that turned Mikey around? What was significant enough to have influenced him to change his actions and, in turn, his life in a very short time frame?

It wasn't any technical skills on how to stand in line better, listen better, lead the group better, be more interested, etc. It wasn't even that I taught him some of the soft people skills like how to be a leader, as he was already leading the class when I met him. He was just leading in the wrong direction.

No, it was simply the fact that I communicated to Mikey that he was someone others could indeed respect. I wanted him to know that he had real potential and that I cared about him. It was the character connection I had made with him that turned his heart home. Respect and care are two of the spokes on the character wheel, which I will introduce in the next few chapters.

When I offered him the chance to be the leader, I was simply channeling his natural leadership abilities into a constructive mode versus the destructive mode he had been leading in life for a long time. Of course, he was just naturally living up to the reputation that others, even teachers, unfortunately, had marked him with previously. I allowed him to believe in himself and know that he could be more and do more with his life!

So, just like Zig (Ziglar) said in *See You at the Top*, "You can have everything in life you want, if you will just help enough other people get what they want."[32] Mikey just needed some care and respect to change his attitude and behavior about life, to feel better about his personal growth, and to respect himself more.

In turn, I became a more significant person in his life and in the lives of the other students I taught, because I had really made a difference in their lives. I literally watched their actions and attitudes change. Guess what?

The next time I came to class, Mikey already had everyone organized, ready, and waiting to start class. I truly had impacted their lives in a very positive way and that is one of the great blessings teachers receive from their jobs in the classrooms of life. As teachers, we are on the front lines of life, making a difference in the lives of our children and, in many ways, for future generations of children to come.

Leading with the heart and living life with character first is the most important commitment we can make in our personal lives and businesses.

5. Value Character over Talent

A few days ago, I reflected on my daily John C. Maxwell devotional (*Leadership Promises for Every Day*), which included leadership promises from the book of Proverbs from the Bible. One of the messages John focused on that caught my attention was from Proverbs 5:22: "The evil deeds of the wicked ensnare them; the cords of their sins hold them fast."[33] It talks about how a person can be trapped by their own sins. This reminded me of how vital character really is, especially in our world today. None of us wants to be trapped, let alone trapped in our own sin.

John emphasizes that so many leaders, whether in politics, business, or religion, stumble morally. We must always remember, as my mentor Lee Ellis would say, that we're just one decision away from a mistake. It all comes down to our choices. *Every action we take is a choice we make.* Therefore, that seat of courage in the Tricycle Effect is vital. It's about making the right choice at the right moment and for the right reasons.

So how do we safeguard ourselves from falling? According to John in his devotional *Leadership Promises for Every Day*, we should prioritize a leader's character over their abilities or gifts.[34]

We sometimes get caught in the trap of unhealthy comparisons. Wishing we had someone else's speed, wealth, job, or position can be an endless and unsatisfying pursuit. Social media doesn't make it easier either. When we watch the highlight reel of others, it's easy to get discouraged with every post—and then there are the ads placed in our face to encourage us to desire more and compare ourselves to others.

But remember, these cravings can be unhealthy. We are who we are, created in God's image, and we should find peace and satisfaction in that. It's crucial that we *call out to the designer: value and reward character above talents.* John suggests that we need to nurture both our talents and our character and find a balanced approach. This idea ties back to the Tricycle Effect and the competence skills wheels, which also talks about the wheel sizes being balanced—a concept borrowed from gymnastics.

By focusing on nurturing both aspects and leading with character first, we set ourselves and others up for genuine success. We pave the way to finish strong, to lead others effectively, and most importantly, to lead ourselves well.

Always remember, my friend, to lead and coach yourself first. Once you've managed that, you'll be well positioned to lead and coach others with character first, steering them from mere success to true significance.

Trike on!

6. Better Mentoring Abilities

Coach-ability can also lead to better mentoring abilities. By being open to feedback and constructive criticism, mentors can identify areas for improvement and develop new skills and strategies. Coach-ability can also help mentors adapt to changes and new challenges in the mentoring relationship, which can lead to better outcomes for their mentees.

As a dad and coach, I have always realized that even though I had children growing up under my protection and guidance, sometimes I had to take a time-out from my role as a dad and coach for my own children and instead play the role of mentor.

The definition of *mentor* according to Dictionary.com is "a wise and trusted counselor or teacher."[35] I think a mentor is someone who will tell you what you need to hear to guide you in learning something new. A mentor is more about the head than the heart, like the roles of dad and coach. I know there is a fine line I walk when I say that, but I think the mentor is separated emotionally from the mentee as a dad or coach might be connected emotionally.

Let me share a story with you that will help you understand the complexity of balancing roles in life as coach, mentor, and dad: it involves Moses (my second-oldest son), gymnastics judges, and moments for teaching character in motion.

During my son Moses's gymnastics journey, his ability to be coached became very evident. He had some natural talent and was hungry to excel in his sport. For many years, Moses engaged intensively in various activities, including gymnastics, tumbling, and trampoline, at both the local and national levels. When faced with the choice between focusing on gymnastics or tumbling and trampoline, he chose the latter, eventually reaching the incredible milestone of representing the United States at the world championships on trampoline.

Interestingly, during those formative years, I had the privilege of being his coach while also navigating the dynamic of being his dad. Moses and I would oscillate between our father-son relationship and coach-athlete relationship, a dance that sometimes meant keeping these roles distinctly separate. Remarkably, Moses never openly complained about me being both his coach and dad, demonstrating a level of respect and patience that I greatly admired.

Throughout our shared journey, my coaching strategy encompassed not only technical advice about how to jump on a trampoline or leadership and interpersonal skills but also character development. One memorable instance still vividly stands out, which occurred during a parallel bars event at one of the men's gymnastics competitions.

Observing an evident error in judgment by an official, Moses and I approached the judge to inquire about that specific situation. I was about to step out of my role as dad and coach to confront the judge, holding him accountable and allowing Moses to assume the role as mentee.

I even prepped Moses and told him to listen and watch carefully because I was about to teach him something that he could learn, which was important and would contribute to a character-values teaching moment.

This mentoring moment began with a straightforward query to the judge: Why hadn't a deduction been assigned when a coach visibly assisted a gymnast during their routine? Instead of acknowledging the apparent lapse in judgment or explaining a missed call, the judge chose to respond, "I gave him the benefit of the doubt."

Although the infraction was clear—the coach clearly held the gymnast's hand—the judge leaned on subjectivity and autonomy to validate his decision, essentially enabling and indirectly encouraging a violation of the rules.

While it would have been understandable to challenge this apparent miscarriage of justice, I chose instead to express gratitude to the judge for his time and explanation. Moses, attentively observing the exchange, witnessed not only the unfairness of the judgment in this situation but, more importantly, my response to it. No emotion on my part. Simply the facts.

I think the dad in me would have been very emotional and wanted fairness for his son. But I think the coach in me would have wanted justice for the lack of character judgment in favor of the competition.

However, it was the mentor in me that could set up the learning moment and, without the emotion of a dad or coach, be a neutral observer as a mentor and help the mentee to learn a tremendously valuable lesson in sportsmanship and character values.

When Moses and I discussed the incident afterward, it became apparent that he understood the complex layers of what had transpired. He recognized the blatant infraction on the part of the coach to cheat and the judge to provide the benefit of the doubt when there really was no doubt. But perhaps more significantly, he learned from my measured and respectful response as a mentor to the judge's flawed character-values decision.

Our young ones observe and absorb our actions, even when we might not realize it. In this particular instance, Moses learned that maintaining respect, even in the face of apparent injustice, is a fundamental aspect of character. I believed it was my job to mentor him at that specific moment in time.

It is so important to lead and influence others with character first. It's not only about technical skills and people skills but also about developing and upholding your character skills. So, as we navigate through our coaching endeavors, we all need to stay grounded in our character, ensuring that it steers our interactions and decision-making and helps us journey to our true north, guided by our moral compass.

In conclusion, coach-ability is a critical trait for personal and professional growth. By being coach-able, individuals can achieve their goals, unlock their full potential, and make a positive impact in their personal and professional lives. Coach-ability can lead to faster personal and professional growth, improved relationships with others, higher job satisfaction and career success, improved leadership skills, and better mentoring abilities. By developing coach-ability, individuals can make significant strides toward achieving their goals and fulfilling their potential.

In your coaching endeavors, remain open, stay coach-able, and always, trike on!

Chalk Talk Coaching Tip

Coach-ability accelerates personal and professional growth, serving as a foundation for values-driven leadership and fostering quicker achievement of goals. Embracing feedback, nurturing character skills, and leading with integrity are essential for cultivating strong relationships and steering toward a life marked by success and significance.

- **Promise of solution**: Embracing coach-ability can accelerate your growth by intentionally cultivating a mindset that values continual learning and adaptability, leading to enhanced performance and fulfillment both personally and professionally.

- **Suggested action step**: Set a weekly goal to seek out feedback in one specific area of your work or personal life. Reflect on this feedback, identify actionable steps you can take to improve, and integrate those steps into your daily routine. This habit of seeking and applying feedback will foster your coach-ability and contribute to your growth.

Workbook for Coach-Ability, Chapter 5

The Benefits of Coach-Ability—Coach-Leader

Fill-in-the-Blanks

1. Coach-ability can help individuals develop a growth mindset, which can help them overcome obstacles, achieve their goals more quickly, and improve their _____ skills.

2. By being open to feedback and constructive criticism, individuals can improve their ability to listen actively and _____ effectively.

3. John C. Maxwell highlights that character is the _____ of leadership, showing its foundational role in effective leadership.

Reflective Questions

1. Can you think of a situation where being open to feedback led to a noticeable improvement in your

personal or professional life? What was the feedback, and how did it help you grow?

2. Reflect on a time when you prioritized character over talent or skill. How did this decision affect the outcome and relationships involved?

3. How does the idea of leading with character first resonate with you, and in what ways can you apply this principle in your daily interactions both at work and in your personal life?

Summary of Chapter 5 Workbook

Chapter 5 of the workbook invites readers to explore the multifaceted benefits of coach-ability, emphasizing that it leads not only to personal and professional development but also lays the groundwork for values-driven leadership. The fill-in-the-blanks questions aim to reinforce the key concepts discussed in the chapter, such as the importance of character in leadership and the impact of effective communication. Reflective questions prompt readers to apply these ideas to their own experiences, encouraging introspection on how coach-ability has influenced their growth trajectory and relationships. By contemplating instances where character took precedence over talent and considering the principle of leading with character first, readers are guided to appreciate the profound influence of coach-ability on their path to success and significance.

Part 2:

Coaching Yourself

CHAPTER 6
How to Develop Coach-Ability
COACH YOURSELF FIRST

Integrity is the glue that holds our way of life together....When wealth is lost, nothing is lost; when health is lost, something is lost; when character is lost, all is lost. — Billy Graham[36]

AS WE ARE LEARNING, being coach-able is a critical trait for personal and professional success. In this chapter, we will explore some ways to develop coach-ability, including setting learning goals and seeking feedback, active listening and asking clarifying questions, embracing a growth mindset, developing resilience and adaptability, and practicing patience and persistence. Sometimes our words do not match our meaning, and this keeps us from truly understanding what counts in life.

> **Challenge/Problem statement:** Developing coach-ability is often impeded by a lack of self-reflection and self-direction, leaving individuals unprepared to fully engage in their own growth.

Did you know that principles are not the same as values? Principles, like gravity or centrifugal force, are outside of our body and outside our control.

However, values comprise our internal values. Sometimes, we refer to those internal values as character values, which are who we really are. Sometimes, values are in harmony with the decisions we make, and sometimes, the values conflict with each other. So, it is imperative that we lead from the heart, live with character first, and launch our life" forward with values.

Let me give you an example. How would you answer this question?

Character values like integrity and loyalty are important, but which is more important?

When discussing the importance of character values like integrity and loyalty, it's important to note that both values play significant roles in leadership and have their own unique importance. However, determining which is more important can be subjective and depend on the specific context and circumstances. Let's explore each value individually:

- **Integrity:** Integrity is often considered a foundational character value in leadership. It refers to the consistency between your actions, values, and principles. Leaders who prioritize integrity demonstrate honesty, transparency, and ethical behavior. They consistently align with their values and make decisions based on what is morally right. Integrity builds trust, credibility, and respect among team members, stakeholders, and the broader community.

- **Loyalty:** Loyalty, however, refers to a strong sense of commitment, support, and faithfulness toward individuals or causes. In a leadership context, loyalty typically involves being dedicated to the team, organization, its mission, and the people within it. Loyalty can manifest as support during challenging times, standing up for team members, and fostering a sense of unity and collaboration. It helps to build a positive and cohesive work culture.

Both integrity and loyalty are vital for effective leadership, and they often go hand in hand. Integrity establishes a leader's ethical leadership foundation, while loyalty fosters a sense of trust and commitment within the team. It's challenging to pinpoint which is more important, as they are interrelated and complement each other. Fortunately, we don't have to decide based merely on importance alone since they both work together in harmony with one another. A leader with integrity inspires loyalty, while a loyal leader upholds their integrity.

Ultimately, leaders should strive to cultivate both integrity and loyalty. These character values are not mutually exclusive, and by embodying both, leaders can create a strong workplace environment, as well as a culture of trust, transparency, and unity. The key is finding the right balance that aligns with the culture, as the specific needs and values of the organization and the character of the individual leaders involved need to match.

So is there ever a time when integrity should be more important than loyalty?

Yes, there can be situations where integrity should take precedence over loyalty. While loyalty is an important value in leadership, there are instances where maintaining your integrity and ethical principles is of utmost importance. Here are a few scenarios where integrity may outweigh loyalty:

- **Ethical dilemmas:** When faced with ethical dilemmas, it is crucial for leaders to prioritize integrity over loyalty. Upholding moral principles and doing what is right should take precedence, even if it means going against the interests or wishes of individuals or the organization.

- **Unethical practices:** If loyalty requires participating in or condoning unethical practices, it is vital for leaders to choose integrity. Engaging in activities that compromise integrity can damage your reputation, credibility, and the trust of stakeholders. Upholding ethical standards is paramount for sustainable success.

- **Legal compliance:** If loyalty involves engaging in activities that violate laws and regulations, integrity should always prevail. Complying with legal obligations is essential for maintaining ethical standards, preserving the organization's reputation, and safeguarding the well-being of employees and stakeholders.

- **Protecting the greater good:** In situations where loyalty to a specific individual or group conflicts with the greater good or the interests of the larger organization, leaders should prioritize integrity. This may involve making difficult decisions that prioritize the well-being and long-term success of the organization and its stakeholders.

It is essential to remember that integrity and loyalty are not mutually exclusive, and in most cases, they can coexist harmoniously. However, when faced with situations where integrity and loyalty come into conflict, it is crucial for leaders to prioritize acting with integrity and upholding ethical values. This demonstrates strong moral leadership and fosters trust, transparency, and long-term success.

Just as a person's personality should reflect their character, the culture in a business should reflect the character of the leadership in that organization or business as well. As they say, "People don't leave companies; people leave people."

I like to shape that quote into something a little different to add even more meaning: When the character of the people in a company's workforce does not align with the character of the people in the leadership of that company, people leave the culture of the company.

The main reason for that is that each person in a company or organization is a leader, no matter the stature, rank, or position of that individual. Each person plays a part and role in the company's culture.

As John C. Maxwell says, "Leadership is influence, nothing more, nothing less."[37] That definition means that each person influences others in the company or organization. And why is that?

A person's character is the primary influence in the culture of that company, no matter how great or small. So, regardless of power or position, rank or stature, each person's character adds to and multiplies the effect of the company or organizational culture—the very heartbeat of business and life.

1. Setting Learning Goals and Seeking Feedback

One of the best ways to develop coach-ability is to set learning goals and actively seek feedback. Be accountable by identifying areas for improvement and seeking feedback from others. Individuals can identify areas of strength and weakness and work toward continual self-improvement.

When seeking feedback or even listening to feedback from others, we need to filter out the productive and constructive feedback.

This story illustrates feedback from someone who should have been a leader with character but instead focused on the technical skills wheel at the expense of the people skills wheel and, most importantly, the character skills wheel.

An Unexpected, "Disgusting" Encounter

Let's delve into a peculiar event that happened to me involving a gymnast whose parents I had never met. One day while at a local store, I spotted one of our gymnasts with a couple who I assumed were her parents. Eagerly, I nudged my wife, Kathy, suggesting we introduce ourselves. This gymnast was relatively new to our gym, so we were still in the early stages of getting to know her.

Upon introducing Kathy and myself to her parents, her dad asked me, "Are you the guy from the radio?" Affirming that I was the guy he heard being interviewed by the radio talk show host, I nodded, and he proceeded, "The one always talking about character?" Again, I affirmed. Then, without hesitation, he declared, "You're disgusting."

I was taken aback, especially since he was bold enough to label me "disgusting" in front of his daughter, whom we fondly referred to as our gym daughter, a term we use lovingly for all our gymnasts. It left me pondering: How could someone label me, a stranger, who primarily spoke about positive character traits like caring, trustworthiness, and responsibility on the radio as disgusting? It made me wonder if perhaps I'd inadvertently struck a nerve.

I am using this story to illustrate how feedback from others could be very hurtful and even detrimental to how someone feels about themselves and could even affect their ability to build healthy relationships.

How should I have reacted? In my own mind, how should I frame this feedback that I received? What should my response be in terms of self-talk and self-coaching after receiving this kind of labeling from someone?

Those are all great questions, and many of us have an opportunity to ask those questions after receiving feedback that might be judgmental and even nonproductive. In addition, once we ask these questions in our heads, our hearts and brains then go about processing the questions and formulating answers.

As a coaching moment, I want to walk you through my response, my questions, and the answers in my self-talk coaching to help me process and respond to this feedback.

First, I did not react in any way when this person said I was disgusting. I simply acted as if I'd never heard what they said. I was able to do that because immediately, my brain said, Don't react, only respond. Reaction is often a knee jerk or emotion on the spur of the moment, whereas response is a conscious decision to respond without emotion. So my response, without missing a beat, was to ask this dad where he worked. I had basically turned the conversation around to focus on the person who had made the remark. I cannot tell you why I responded that way, except that I am sure I have not responded like that always. I am human just like you, and just as we have discussed with the human factor, I am not perfect. But I am a human becoming on this journey we call life together with you.

Maybe my mind processed it very quickly since I had never met this person. Therefore, I immediately disregarded the comment as over the top. Nevertheless, by not reacting and only responding, I think you would agree that I demonstrated good character. In this case, thinking of this person versus my own possible hurt or disappointment and reacting was the right thing to do.

Second, even though this young gymnast was his biological daughter, she was my gym daughter, and as her "gym dad," I answered my own question. I consciously thought, I need to make sure I set a good example for her. That kind of thinking results from practicing daily character habits for personal growth and the day-to-day study of leading with character first in life.

Now, I am not perfect. In a different setting, and if this dad had pressed me any further by calling me out in some other way, I might have chosen to respond differently, but I definitely would have responded and not reacted. What caused me to make that decision? I was in the tricycle seat, and I intuitively knew, from all the study and practice on leading and living with character, that I needed to make the right decision at the right time and for the right reason. That is such a nice philosophy, isn't it? Except, for me, it is *not* a philosophy. It is who I am, and this is my daily grind. I hope reading this book and allowing me to coach you will make it your daily habit and grind as well. I live knowing I will always be called on to make courageous decisions, but our culture and society today do not always consistently reward tough, courageous decisions like in days of old. Instead, I choose to reward myself for my courage, and decisiveness, and to simply chalk up another win for a character-driven life. Practice makes perfect, even when we are practicing leadership with character and values.

Third, my thoughts really did turn to the dad. Have you ever heard the phrase *hurting people hurt people*? I suspect this dad, so quick to judge my character, may have been lacking in his own character. His reaction suggested resistance to messages about caring, relationship building, and overall people skills—all things essential to fostering healthy environments and relationships. His brash statement only fueled my determination and resolve to continue promoting character-driven leadership and messages in the future. But at that moment, turning the conversation to him and asking him questions to show my interest in his life definitely took the edge off the whole situation.

How about you? How would you have handled this situation? Can you see the self-talk that resulted from coaching myself with character-driven decisions? Coaching myself allowed me to respond and not react. There are real benefits to conflict management, relationship building, leadership, and much more if we focus on leading with character skills and values first in life.

You see, over the years, instead of using my radio time to promote my company directly, I have chosen to coach listeners on character. I might have opted to advertise more about our offerings, urging listeners to buy our services, but I saw a more profound opportunity to influence listeners through the lens of character and values-driven leadership, in order to add value and make a difference for them.

Though that dad's feedback was harsh, it wasn't the only feedback we received. Over the years, countless individuals, some even several hours away, reached out, appreciative of our radio messages promoting the necessity of character in leadership.

So, my encouragement to you today is this: Never underestimate your influence. Filter the feedback you get to coach yourself and discover if something is constructive or destructive, then treat the destructive feedback for what it is. Just as I coach my gymnasts who may have screwed up on a routine in a meet or not met their goals on any one particular skill or day, treat that experience as if it never even happened. That is the essence of coaching yourself to be kind and caring, even to yourself.

Remember, when it doesn't seem apparent, or that you are making a difference, your words and actions may very well be making an everlasting impact. In your heart of hearts, you know. I believe that all my stories and discussions across the airwaves on the radio about character and leading with character first more than likely challenged this dad and his personal philosophy and actions in life. So, I encourage you not to think ill of people who might call you out in an unprofessional manner sometimes. Again, I am reminded that hurting people hurt people. Somehow this person was hurting, and I hope that in later years, when he may need it most, he will remember one of my messages about character and adding significance in life. Remember that we all have only one life to live, and after that, we die. Let me ask you this question: What did you do in this life to be significant to others by helping them to have joy in the journey? It is not too late, you know. You can start coaching yourself today to *live a legacy*, not just *leave a legacy*.

Be kind, my friend, we only pass through this life one time.

> "I shall pass this way but once; any good that I can do or any kindness I can show to any human being; let me do it now. Let me not defer nor neglect it, for I shall not pass this way again." — Anonymous quote, popularly attributed to Étienne de Grellet[3]

Keep striving, remain coach-able, guide others and, most importantly, filter the feedback by coaching yourself with character first, then accept the constructive feedback with your self-coaching to make a meaningful difference for yourself and in the lives of others.

It takes a mature person of character to offset the negative in life and stay on course heading true north with your moral compass.

Stay coach-able, friend, and trike on!

2. Active Listening and Asking Clarifying Questions

Active listening is a critical skill for being coach-able. It means paying attention to what the coach or mentor is saying and trying to understand their perspective. Active listening also involves asking clarifying questions and seeking to understand the feedback being provided.

I love Stephen R. Covey's idea: We don't listen to hear—we listen to respond. That is a paraphrase of a quote from Stephen R. Covey's *The 7 Habits of Highly Effective People*: "Most people do not listen with the intent to understand; they listen with the intent to reply."[39]

The Silent Power of Listening

During officer school when I was at Maxwell Air Force Base, our squadron, a mix of around 20 male and female officers, faced a challenging training event. Our task involved moving from one part of our base to another and planting explosives at a target within a set time frame. The journey was anything but smooth. We had to carry the heaviest member on a stretcher, ensuring no one was left behind. Throughout, paintball snipers took out some of our members, thinning our ranks.

The real challenge arose when an unexpected, towering wall blocked our path in a forested area. With no way around the wall, we had to scale it. A disagreement splintered our already reduced team of five into two smaller groups, one a group of three men, the other a female officer and myself. The three men, prioritizing speed, abandoned us, climbing over the wall and dashing ahead without a backward glance. Left with no other option, the female officer and I teamed up, carefully leveraging each other to scale the wall.

Once we overcame this obstacle, two paths lay before us: a direct route across an open field directly to the target or a more hidden path through the woods. I hesitated, leaning toward the concealed-woods route, but my companion, quietly confident, suggested the straightforward and more direct across the open field path. Trusting her intuition over my initial reluctance, we ventured across the field. As it turned out, this was the wisest choice. The three men who'd abandoned us lay "dead," victims of the simulated enemy snipers, along the edge of the woodsy path.

The officer's quiet intuition had led us to success, defying the might and confidence of our physically stronger teammates. We completed the training mission, one of the few teams to do so, thanks to her silent wisdom and my choice to listen.

The lesson? The quiet, often-overlooked voice can hold unexpected insight and moral strength. In my years of coaching and teaching, I've consistently found that the unassuming, silent individual frequently harbors perspectives that can shift paradigms and guide a team to success.

Listening—truly listening—requires an embracing silence to hear those soft-spoken voices. It's an art that's not always easy to master. Sometimes we succeed, and sometimes we forget and need a gentle reminder. The alignment of *listen* and *silent* serves as my reminder to honor the silence, be present, and genuinely hear those quiet voices that may very well lead us to our objectives.

Remember, listen and silent have the exact same letters.

If I had not allowed my teammate to coach me and, in turn, coach myself to accept her advice, we would not have been successful. Trust in others and trust in your own self-talk coaching is so important. If we are constantly guided by our moral conscience and character, we will most often coach ourselves to the right goal and destination. Self-coaching does not mean there is no outside input. Self-coaching is most successful and significant when we accept feedback and coaching from others and then make the final coaching decision for ourselves.

And so, my friends, remain coach-able and remember that sometimes the strength we need to triumph isn't in the loudest shout but in the gentlest whisper. Stay coach-able and trike on!

3. Embracing a Growth Mindset

A growth mindset is the belief that your abilities can be developed through hard work and dedication. Embracing a growth mindset can help individuals view challenges and setbacks as opportunities for learning and growth rather than as obstacles.

Sometimes our greatest obstacles might be within ourselves.

Embracing a growth mindset, even if the greatest obstacles in life might be something we are born with, is another way we can influence others by leading with character first. After all, character levels the playing field. The naturally talented and those gifted with high IQ with their competence skills wheels must lead with character first as well, or they'll fail at moving in life from success to significance. Against all odds, we overcome these kinds of obstacles with a healthy growth mindset.

To illustrate this idea that character trumps competence, I want to share a story of triumph through character.

Growing up as the child of an Air Force member, my life was a mosaic of new places and experiences all the time. From the time I was born in the Mojave Desert on Edwards Air Force Base to seven years in California to a brief six-month stint in Washington, DC, and eventually four years in Venezuela, every move brought new adventures. In Venezuela, I formed a special friendship with a boy named Tony, who had cerebral palsy from birth. Despite his physical limitations, Tony exhibited a remarkable spirit, always embracing life and its various opportunities. He always seemed happy and content, which I saw as strange but remarkable.

Tony and I shared classes, adventures, and numerous trips, exploring beautiful beaches and locations thanks to his dad's corporate plane trips together. Our bond was a blend of play, genuine companionship, and deep mutual respect. We simply enjoyed being in each other's company and having fun together.

One day in Caracas, at our school, known as Escuela Campo Alegre, we faced a physical challenge. In our physical education class, we were tasked with running around the football field within a set time frame. For Tony, this was an especially formidable challenge due to his physical disability, which rendered half of his body nearly nonfunctional. When he ran, his arm curled inward, and he dragged one foot, yet his resolve was undeterred.

While others completed their laps and dispersed, Tony persisted, completing only about a third of the field when everyone else was finished. I, having finished my lap, decided that leaving Tony to struggle alone was not an option. I retraced my steps, joining him to encourage, walk, and run alongside him, ensuring he was not alone. Tony and I finished the run together. While he might not have met the set time, neither of us cared. The victory lay in finishing the race, not in the time taken.

There's a profound lesson embedded in this memory: The journey and its completion often outweigh the speed of attainment or the finish line. Sometimes, what we are called to do might stretch beyond our physical capabilities or mental readiness. However, the determination to fulfill our purpose propels us beyond our limitations. I was immensely proud of Tony, who defied his physical constraints to achieve his goal. I admired him and still do!

My friends, I extend this encouragement to you: even when you confront seemingly insurmountable obstacles, with goals set far or bars set high above your reach, remember Tony. If it aligns with your desire, purpose, mission, and heartfelt yearning, you can achieve it. Embrace the spirit of "believe it, dream it, do it." Keep reminding yourself with your self-talk coaching that your purpose, your passion, and your mission are what really count. Keep your heart, head, and eyes on your true north, and refer to your moral compass often.

Search for the Tonys in your life—those who may need that extra boost of encouragement from you or a companion to walk beside them through challenges. It wasn't about success in the run—it was about being significant in Tony's life, reminding us to prioritize making meaningful impacts in the lives of others. Servant leadership (influence) is the perfect coach-leader.

Keep serving others first while leading with character first, and you will journey from success to significance, my friend!

Trike on!

4. Resilience and Adaptability

Developing resilience and adaptability are essential for being coach-able. Resilience is the ability to bounce back from setbacks, while adaptability is the ability to adjust to changing circumstances. By developing these skills, individuals can learn to embrace challenges and setbacks as opportunities for growth and learning. Resilience and adaptability are two more spokes on the people skills wheel, which is one of the two wheels that make up the competence wheels in the Tricycle Effect.

Resilience and Adaptability Work as a Team

Resilience and adaptability are like two friends working together. Sometimes they team up, and other times they do their own thing. Being resilient means you can adjust and recover to get through tough events. Adaptability means you change things up when needed. Not every situation requires changes, depending on the risks and opportunities.

I want to share a story that shows both resilience and adaptability. Some say we shouldn't talk about politics, sex, or religion, but these are part of our lives, right? It's good to talk about them respectfully and learn from each other's experiences.

In 2010, I was running for state senate and broke the rule about not talking politics. I tweeted to show it's about the person's character, not just their political party. I tweeted about two leaders, Lincoln and Hitler, saying one had great character and the other evil. This tweet caused a big stir. The media only reported half the story, making it seem as if I supported Hitler, which I didn't.

This situation could have ruined my campaign, but after the truth was reported, we had even more people joining us on our campaign. You see, our campaign for state senate was all about the people and not the party. I stuck to my values and kept campaigning as if it never even happened. In the end, I lost the election by a narrow margin, but I learned a lot. I stayed true to myself, showing that sticking to your values is key to resilience.

After the campaign, an interesting thing happened. My daughter met someone at a wedding who had spread my tweet. He told her that my campaign was the best-run campaign they had ever seen in Washington, DC. Since he was from the opposing political party, he had been tasked with digging up dirt on me and was surprised that the tweet was the only dirt he found on me. It proved my point: character counts. My infamous tweet is the fifth most controversial tweet in history! You can read all about it in *TIME* magazine.[40]

Time Magazine Tweet Headlines

So, remember to focus on a character-driven life and stick to your core values. They guide you like a compass, helping you stay true to yourself. That's how you stay resilient and adaptable, always finding your way back to your true north. Keep trikin' strong!

Adaptability Enhances Resilience!

Adaptability is really important, just like resilience. They can work together, but they're also different. As a gymnastics coach, I know about being flexible—in gymnastics and in adapting to work with each athlete.

Every athlete in our gym is unique. They have their own character and personality. Did you know that our personality is pretty much the same as when we were children?[41] But our character can grow and change over time.

In our gym, we focus on the Tricycle Effect, and character skills are super important. We have banners from Character Counts for trustworthiness, respect, responsibility, fairness, caring, and citizenship (loyalty).[42] https://charactercounts.org/We also teach kids people skills like communication, teamwork, leadership, and problem-solving. And, of course, we teach technical gymnastics skills too!

Kids have different personalities, and they're growing their character skills. So, we adapt our coaching for each of them. One athlete might learn a gymnastics move, like a kip, quickly. Others might need more attempts. Some athletes learn by watching, others by listening, and some by feeling the move. This is where adaptability comes in. We listen and connect with each athlete so they can learn the best way for them.

Adaptability isn't just for sports—it's important in business and life too. Life throws us lots of surprises, and we have to consider things like our families, jobs, and money. Being adaptable helps us handle these surprises, especially when we lead with good character. Adaptability enhances resilience by allowing us to be able to handle any event, circumstance, or situation.

We show the athletes in the gym that we care about them and won't give up on them. We don't want them to give up on themselves either, so we teach them how to be adaptable in many situations. We help them learn to set goals, prepare, practice, and ultimately perform their routines in competitions. We even teach them how to fail gracefully, as if it never even happened. Practicing skills, putting them in a routine, and performing their routines in competitions are all different situations, and being adaptable helps in each step.

One of the most important skills we teach in the gym is to treat success and failure the same. The reason is that athletes learn to be resilient through their adaptability. For instance, if an athlete does poorly on uneven bars during their first event at a meet, instead of them crying and feeling sorry for themselves, we teach them to shake it off and move on to the next event, as if it never even happened.

The world can sometimes feel chaotic. Whether it's COVID, the economy, or life challenges, staying adaptable is super important and truly enhances our ability to be and stay resilient. So, let's stay adaptable and keep being resilient!

Trike on!

Adaptability Can Stand Alone

Let's talk more about adaptability even further as a key people skill. For about 18 years, our gymnastics training center also taught adaptive physical education. We've worked with many individuals, including those with Down syndrome, spinal cord injuries, brain injuries, cerebral palsy, and other learning disabilities. Exercise can really help with healing and communication.

One time, we had a student named Danny (not his real name). Danny was overweight and nonverbal, plus he struggled with his hearing. He attended formal speech therapy classes to learn to speak, but progress was slow. During sessions in our gym, I focused on helping Danny get physically fit. I got an idea to help Danny with pull-ups. I thought this might strengthen his arms as part of his overall physical fitness.

As I assisted Danny, I realized that if I put my arms under his armpits to support him, I could actually help him do pull-ups. Inadvertently, each time we did pull-ups, I had my cheek against his ear. I would count our repetitions, and over several sessions, as I counted each pull-up, Danny started to make sounds too. I would say, "One." Danny would say, "Huuun." I would say, "Two." Danny would say, "Whooooo." He started to make sounds!

It was incredible—he hadn't made sounds like this before for us or anyone, even the speech therapist. He had been totally nonverbal. It finally dawned on me that he was feeling the vibrations of my voice on my cheek next to his ear. This was a breakthrough.

Each week, we practiced more. Counting to 10 during pull-ups helped Danny start to speak. He began to say words like *hello* and *goodbye*. It turned out he couldn't hear well, but he could feel vibrations. This discovery allowed us to adapt our exercises to improve his verbal skills. It was an amazing discovery by chance, but we adapted the exercises to enhance his ability to talk and communicate with others.

This experience showed how adaptability can stand alone and can work together in surprising ways. Our adaptability led to a huge improvement in Danny's quality of life. Adaptability isn't just a skill—it can even create miracles.

So, remember the power of being adaptable in life. Let's keep trikin' strong, team!

Patience and Persistence

Developing coach-ability requires patience and persistence to be resilient. It takes time and effort to develop new skills, even character skills, and change behaviors. By practicing patience and persistence, we can stay committed to our goals and continue working toward self-improvement, even in the face of obstacles. The ultimate sign of resilience.

The Power of Focus and Coach-Ability

In my coaching journey, one particular experience with Moses (my second-oldest son) underscored how pivotal the essence of patience and persistence is. I like to say that patience plus persistence plus focus equals resilience. One competitive situation perfectly illustrated the power of patience plus persistence plus focus, which leads to resilience.

Moses, excelling as an elite level 10 trampolinist, needed higher-level coaching from elite instructors, often requiring travel to specialized facilities in the Twin Cities to accommodate advanced-training needs. Our local gym, despite having the tallest building available when we established it, couldn't suffice for his increasingly complex routines and high bounces, especially with trampoline work.

Moses was competing at a critical regional trampoline meet in Rockford, Illinois, that served as a gateway to qualifying for national competition.

In trampoline events, athletes perform a compulsory routine followed by an optional one, each preceded by its own respective warm-up. Moses finished his compulsory warm-up and started his competitive compulsory routine when he surprisingly executed a full twist instead of the mandatory layout on his first trick, instantaneously invalidating the routine per the rules. He received a zero for a score.

His heartfelt disappointment was palpable. He'd worked hard all year to qualify for this regional meet and traveled eight hours to participate in this competition. Now, it was over in less than one minute. Failure and opportunity to learn. I never saw Moses cry, and he never said much about that moment at all. He simply acted as if it never even happened. Of course, that is how we trained him, and his character acted it out perfectly.

Surprisingly, the judges acknowledged his initial misstep and offered him a second chance, which is definitely against the rulebook. Therefore, in a decisive moment of instilling a crucial lesson of focus for my son, I declined, choosing to respect the established rules despite the judges being willing to bend them. Moses erred and failed at that moment, and the ensuing consequence was a bitter pill that needed swallowing if he was to learn that failure is simply an event, not a person, and is part of learning to focus and be resilient. It was a lesson not just in gymnastics but in life and character building: adhere to the rules, focus, and live with the outcomes, whether triumphing in success or disheartening in failure.

This lesson bore significant fruit in subsequent competitions a few years later during the trampoline and tumbling national competition held at Disney's inaugural Wide World of Sports event. Despite facing really strong competition, Moses was focused and resilient, and he diligently completed his routines without becoming intimidated by the talent of his competitors. He concentrated on his performance, doing precisely what he knew, what he had practiced, and what was required. The result was a triumphant success: a bronze medal, placing third nationally amid an incredibly talented cohort.

The medal, while shiny and indicative of his physical prowess, symbolized so much more. It represented the unseen yet invaluable lesson learned in Rockford. Focus, adherence to rules, and the acceptance of consequences, even in their harshest form, had fortified Moses with resilience, mental toughness, and emotional strength. This experience equipped him for future challenges, both in and out of the gym.

This series of competition events really brings home the need for unwavering focus, steadfast patience, and persistence to build resilience—not only in the sporting arena but in all facets of life.

Today, Moses is a very talented lieutenant colonel in the U.S. Army and is raising a very healthy family.

So, as we pedal through our respective journeys, we need good focus to remain persistent, patient, and coach-able so we can nurture our endeavors, dreams, and character skills with resilience. As John C. Maxwell coaches, this path defines high road leaders, or in my words, those leading with character skill values with the Tricycle Effect become *high character-driven leaders*.[43]

In conclusion, developing coach-ability requires a combination of different skills and attitudes, including setting learning goals and seeking feedback, listening actively, and asking clarifying questions, embracing a growth mindset, developing resilience and adaptability, and practicing patience and persistence. By developing these skills, individuals can become more coach-able and achieve greater success in their personal and professional lives.

In our journey pedaling through life and its myriad of challenges, remember to stay focused, persistent, patient, and most of all, coach-able to be truly resilient.

Trike on!

Chalk Talk Coaching Tip

In this chapter, I emphasize the critical role of self-coaching in personal and professional success, outlining strategies such as setting learning goals, seeking feedback, and practicing active listening to foster growth. I differentiated principles from values, advocating for leading with character values like integrity and loyalty, which underpin authentic and effective leadership.

- **Promise of solution:** By committing to a reflective and proactive approach to personal development, you can unlock the full potential of being coach-able, leading to enhanced personal and professional growth.

- **Suggested action step**: Begin a daily journaling practice to reflect on your actions and decisions and their alignment with your core values. At the end of each day, write down at least one thing you learned, one area for improvement, and one step you can take tomorrow to enact that improvement. This practice will bolster your self-awareness and self-guidance, foundational elements of coach-ability.

Workbook for Coach-Ability, Chapter 6
How to Develop Coach-Ability

Fill-in-the-Blanks

1. Principles like gravity or centrifugal force are outside of our body and outside our control, whereas _____ comprise our values internally.

2. When discussing character values, it is important to note that both _____ and _____ play significant roles in leadership.

3. Being coach-able means first being coach-able and loyal by influencing ourselves through our own _____, _____, _____, _____ and _____.

Reflective Questions

1. Reflect on a time when you faced an ethical dilemma. How did you prioritize your character values, such as integrity and loyalty, in making your decision? How

did this choice reflect your personal commitment to character-driven leadership?

2. Think about a situation where you had to be both resilient and adaptable. What was the challenge, and how did you navigate it? What did this experience teach you about the relationship between resilience, adaptability, and success?

3. Recall a moment when you provided or received feedback that was difficult to hear. How did you process this feedback, and what steps did you take to ensure that you remained coach-able? How did this experience enhance your growth mindset?

Summary of Chapter 6 Workbook

In this chapter, we explored the intrinsic value of being coach-able for both personal and professional growth. We learned that coach-ability extends beyond just being coached by others; it also includes the often-overlooked aspect of coaching ourselves. Setting clear learning goals, actively seeking and processing feedback, engaging in active listening, asking clarifying questions, fostering a growth mindset, building resilience and adaptability, and exercising patience and persistence are all practices that enhance our coach-ability. We also distinguished between principles, which are external forces outside our control, and values, which are internal and define our character. By understanding and embodying character values such as integrity and loyalty, we not only influence others but also guide our own lives toward success and significance, cementing the fact that leadership is fundamentally rooted in character. Character is, indeed, the foundation of leadership.

CHAPTER 7
Barriers to Coach-Ability

Failure is simply the opportunity to begin again more intelligently. — Henry Ford[44]

WE ARE BEGINNING TO understand how important being coach-able is for personal and professional leadership growth. However, many barriers can prevent individuals from being coach-able. In this chapter, we will discuss some of the most common barriers to coach-ability, including fear of failure, resistance to change, lack of self-awareness, lack of accountability, and a fixed mindset.

> **Challenge/Problem statement:** The fear of failure can immobilize individuals, hindering their ability to embrace new experiences and learn from their mistakes, ultimately obstructing personal and professional growth.

1. Fear of Failure

Fear of failure is one of the most common barriers to coach-ability. Individuals who are afraid of failing are often hesitant to take risks or try new things, which can limit their personal growth and leadership development. Overcoming the fear of failure requires you to be intentional and develop a growth mindset to understand that mistakes are opportunities for learning and growth.

As we discussed previously in chapter 5, we need to feel free in failure and remember that as in sports, so too it is in business.

> As Henry Ford says, "Failure is simply the opportunity to begin again more intelligently."[2] Failure is an event, not a person.

In his book, *Chasing Failure* motivational speaker Ryan Leak says, "Chasing failure took me further than chasing success ever did."[46]

I like to say that successful failure—which means being able to process and deal with failure the same as we do success—builds grit and resilience in a way that nothing else can.

We teach our athletes to treat failure and success the same. That means do not get too high when you are successful, and don't allow yourself to get too low when failure occurs. If you treat both the same, you can bomb a gymnastics routine on one event one minute, and the next minute, you are on to the next event and hitting your routine, just as if the failure never happened!

Did you get that? *Like it never happened!*

Let me challenge you with this quote:

Vince Lombardi said, "We are going to relentlessly chase perfection, knowing full well we will not catch it...because in the process we will catch excellence."[47] In gymnastics, we always perform and strive for perfection, that perfect 10. Yet, we know we will never get a perfect 10. But in the striving for perfection, we will have achieved a level of excellence we may never have known had we not chased perfection.

Strive for perfection—achieve excellence!

If you are going to chase failure and not fear it, you must treat failure in your self-talk as if it is a normal part of life in the learning process. Because it is.

So, remember to treat success and failure the same—like it never happened.

Trike on!

2. Resistance to Change

As humans—or better yet, human becomings—none of us likes change. I think it is ingrained in us to dislike change in our lives. Even good changes are still disruptive sometimes, even if the result is not always a failure. Even success can bring about change that we don't necessarily want to embrace.

Change can also be challenging for many people since resistance to change can prevent individuals from being coach-able. Resistance to change can manifest in various ways, including worry, denial, defensiveness, or avoidance. Overcoming resistance to change requires developing a growth mindset, being open to new ideas and perspectives, and being willing to take calculated risks.

This is a *big* obstacle and a huge barrier to coach-ability. Humans hate change. They seem to be happiest in the status quo.

At the Annual Convention and Centennial Observance of the United Brotherhood of Carpenters and Joiners in Chicago, Illinois, in September 1981, President Ronald Reagan said, "Status quo, you know, is Latin for the mess we're in."[48]

That sums up what happens when we stay in the status quo. Everything in life has a cycle, and everything in the universe has a natural tendency to entropy, which is a state of disorder, surprising randomness, and perpetual uncertainty. None of us can stay in one place for very long—there are simply too many variables that come at us each day, whether we like it or not and whether we ask for it or not. We will move either forward or backward to or from our goals in life.

As the saying goes, "Go forward, or go backward, there is no staying the same." Entropy is not our friend. If we quit working to move ahead, we will quickly go backward.

One of our friends, an Olympian in gymnastics, once told my wife that even if he worked for years to peak for the Olympics, without his daily exercise regimen, in two short weeks after the Olympics, his body would revert back to a condition he was in six months prior. That is how quickly our bodies tend to revert back or snap back to a status quo. The interesting part about that is that, like the technical skills wheel, this gymnast trained his body. But there is more to us than our bodies, right? We also have our heads and our hearts. Also, like the people skills wheel, we have to continually work on our people skills, such as relationships, communications, leadership, teamwork, etc.

The people skills are more like your head on your body. And just like the character skills wheel, we must practice our character skills such as trustworthiness, respect, responsibility, fairness, caring, empathy, and loyalty. The character skills are more like your heart in your body. Without regular practice, just as the body can technically return to the status quo or move toward entropy, so can your people skills with your head and your character skills with your heart.

Here is the same image of a tricycle we used before, but this time, I include a few more titles that call out the purpose of the wheels:

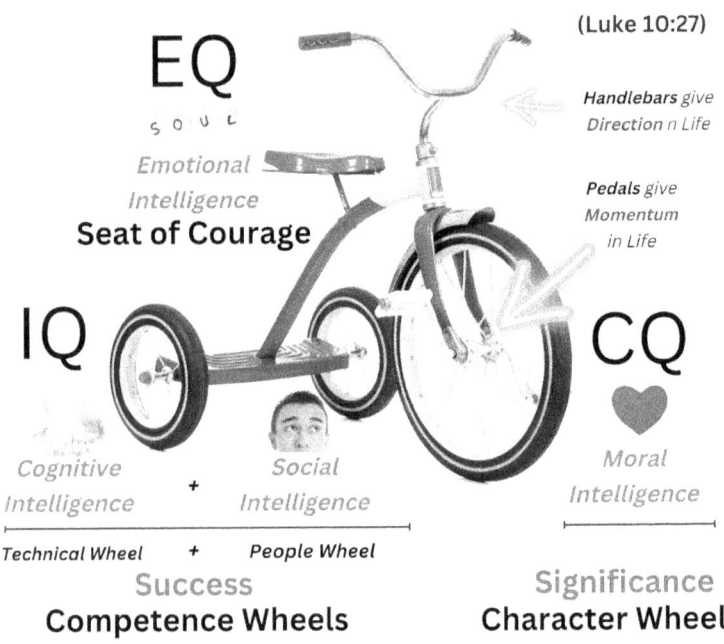

In this image, you can see the summation of the Tricycle Effect:

- Heart is our *moral* intelligence = Character quotient (CQ)

- Head is our *social* intelligence + the body (i.e., hands) is our *cognitive* intelligence = Intelligence quotient (IQ)

- Soul = *Emotional* quotient (EQ)

We need to practice each of these parts of the tricycle equally so we stay balanced in life and grow to fully experience the Tricycle Effect.

When I refer to *practice*, like in physical exercise, I mean that if we want to improve our people skills, we must practice building relationships, improving our communications, honing our leadership and teamwork skills, and so forth. Likewise, even though most people never consciously think about it, we also have to practice our character skills. If we want to be more respectful, we must practice respect. If we want to be more trustworthy, we must practice being more trustworthy. If we want to be more responsible, we must practice responsibility, and so forth. You get the idea. So before we can practice our people skills and character skills, just like our technical skills or the conditioning of our body for exercise and performance, we must first set goals. Without a goal, it will never occur to us that we must practice these skills regularly and intentionally.

So, we must set goals, find our purpose, and pursue it relentlessly. That is the only way to overcome resistance to change and break down the barriers that keep us from becoming coach-able.

Let's get balanced! Trike on!

3. Lack of Self-Awareness

Lack of self-awareness is another barrier to coach-ability. Individuals who lack self-awareness may not recognize their own strengths and weaknesses or be open to feedback. Developing self-awareness requires reflecting on your behaviors and actions, seeking feedback from others, and being open to constructive criticism.

As we have discussed previously, self-talk is not a concept—it is real. We talk to ourselves every day. Let me ask you a question. When was the last time anyone coached you on how you were talking to yourself? My guess is never, or you can't recall a time when someone caught you participating in "naughty talk." In our gym, that is what we call negative self-talk: naughty talk.

Most of our athletes don't understand and are not self-aware of their own self-talk until we start coaching them and helping them with self-talk awareness. We can coach them on it, because, after an attempt at a trick or routine, we hear them say things like *That was awful!* or *Why am I so bad at that?* or *I will never get that trick!* or *I just want to quit!*

Of course, those are just some of the things that we have heard, but all of them have one thing in common: The gymnasts have lost the ability to positively coach themselves when they self-talk like that. They have chosen to self-talk negatively by being negative and even condemning themselves at times. Therefore they make it exceedingly tough to improve during the next attempt at a trick or routine. As Henry Ford also said, "Whether you believe you can do a thing or not, you are right."[49] Our attitudes are shaped by our self-talk, which can be self-prophesying.

We do the same thing as human becomings in our everyday walk of life when we grow up to be adults. If we are judgmental and condemning ourselves, then it is tough to stay flexible in learning and have joy in the journey. Let me say that a little differently with the same meaning. We need to be kind to ourselves and allow ourselves room to make mistakes and not be perfectionistic so that we can find joy in the journey. Our best gymnasts have never been the athletes who were the most talented. The best gymnasts were always the average athlete, who was most hungry and had the most resilience because of their positive self-talk.

Furthermore, if the self-talk comes out audibly so that others hear it, that talk spreads like wildfire if it isn't put out right away. That is especially true when it comes to fear. Self-talk that concerns fear has a tendency to snowball very quickly. One bad statement to ourselves is worth 10 bad statements from someone else. Why is that? you might ask. Think about who is saying it. We never believe we will lie to ourselves, do we? Therefore our self-talk carries way more weight than what someone else might say.

So, the next time you are tempted to beat yourself up with negative self-talk or naughty talk, as we call it in the gym, try being kind to yourself and say something like this: "That was not a good effort, but I will work on this and improve as time goes on." When you talk to yourself that way, you give yourself room to fail and room to improve with no dead end in sight. Then you will have the best opportunity to become your best self and to shoot for the moon, knowing that even if you miss the moon, you will hit the stars. Later in another chapter, we will talk about limiting beliefs and how those limiting beliefs are created through our self-talk but can be overridden to allow us success for ourselves and significance for others in life.

Trike on!

4. Lack of Accountability

Lack of accountability is another barrier to coach-ability. Individuals who are not accountable for their actions may blame others for their mistakes or be resistant to feedback. Overcoming the lack of accountability requires taking ownership of your actions, being open to feedback, and being willing to make changes based on that feedback.

I want to share a story about a notable event in my journey as a student-teacher, an instance that underscored the importance of being coach-able. This event took place during my last semester of college while I was student teaching at the high school I attended when I was growing up. This happened during a spring baseball unit I was teaching as a physical education teacher.

One particular day, as I took attendance on the baseball diamond, I noticed that one student was absent—the star pitcher on the school's baseball team. The school had a clear policy: if a student skips school on the day of a major game, they're not allowed to play in that game. So, naturally, I inquired with the class, wondering if he was sick or something similar, presuming he would certainly know the policy. However, the response I got was unexpected. "Oh, no, he's not sick—he's getting his prom tux."

Perplexed and a bit frustrated, I thought, He skipped class to get his tux for the prom? The confirmation from the class was affirmative, and to add to my surprise, while we were walking back to the school after class, there he was, standing in the window, holding his tux, waving and smiling, as if to taunt me, fully aware of his disregard for the rule.

Knowing that he shouldn't be playing in that night's game, I decided to inform the school counselor, who also served as the baseball coach, assuming that rules were rules and that they would be enforced. This counselor had been my counselor while I was a student there, and I respected him greatly. But, as I relayed the pitcher's violation of the policy, expecting understanding, the counselor erupted with anger, swearing and questioning how I dared to suggest his star pitcher would be benched, even if he skipped class. He blatantly declared the student would play, directly contradicting the school's policy.

Shocked yet undeterred, I escalated the matter to the principal, who had been my vice principal during my school days, and assumed he would enforce the policy. But to my dismay, the principal supported the counselor, also choosing to ignore the established rule. There was no accountability from leadership at two levels. It seemed winning was more important than teaching the importance of this character skill, responsibility. It was so disappointing.

The moral here centers on coach-ability and accountability. This student was not coached to be accountable due to the influential leadership from adults in his life that allowed him to skate by. Those who should have been coaching and enforcing policies chose instead to bypass the rules. Leadership can be a good or bad influence if it is not tied to character skills in the Tricycle Effect. Accountability is a vital skill that can be coached. If rules, policies, or laws are disregarded by those responsible for enforcing them, accountability crumbles, and discipline at all levels suffers.

Moreover, this wasn't just about the student being uncoach-able, but also the two adult leaders in the school who, despite knowing the rules, chose to undermine them, demonstrating their own lack of coach-ability and accountability. They had set a bad example from many angles. It boils down to the importance of character, an element we are discussing throughout this book, *Coach-Ability and the Tricycle Effect*. It is paramount to recognize that good character is to be coach-able, adhere to rules, policies, and regulations, as well as respect those coaching us.

It's crucial to not only follow the rules but also to communicate transparently if and when they are to be bent or broken, explaining why, to avoid setting a precedent that rules can be broken without consequences. That is real accountability. Sadly, many schools and even businesses do not hold their students or employees accountable for poor character. Ensuring we first hold ourselves accountable based on good character skills is key to growing ourselves and coaching others to be champions of character.

So, team, let's always strive to place honor above all and make sure we know, understand, and uphold the rules, policies, and regulations we are bound by, understanding that even when we think no one is watching, someone usually is. If there is a need to deviate from the rules, then we need to make sure that it is communicated and justified based on our moral compass and character skills. Otherwise, we risk undermining our ability to effectively coach ourselves and miss the most important opportunity to coach others and make a difference for them.

Stay accountable and stay coach-able, my friends, and trike on!

5. Fixed Mindset

A fixed mindset is a belief that your abilities and character-istics are fixed and cannot be changed. Individuals with a fixed mindset may often be resistant to feedback or unwilling to try new things. Developing a growth mindset requires recognizing that abilities can be developed through hard work and dedication and being open to new experiences and perspectives.

This is especially true when it comes to developing and coaching character development. Most of the time, we spend very little time or attention on character development and leading our lives consciously and conscientiously with character first.

As a perfect example of this, we even sometimes have things backward in terms of priorities, and that is what holds us back and nails us into this fixed-mindset position in life. How many times have you heard someone say in business that they are working on their mission, vision, and values? Over the years I have heard that a lot! And in that order: mission, then vision, then values.

Well, that statement is exactly backward. We should be saying values, vision, and mission. Why? Because if we consistently led with our character skills and values, we would then see the vision more clearly and thus carry out the mission more efficiently and effectively.

Instead, we put values last, and that is exactly what is missing or misplaced in most any organizations, businesses, or families today if they are not leading with character values first.

Lead with character skill values first, my friend, and you will develop personally and professionally, as well as help coach and mentor your family and business or organizational culture to grow in the healthiest way possible, which will lead to all the physical rewards, such as positive cash flow, return on assets, strong culture in terms of customer service, stronger teams, business longevity, and so much more.

Remember that character and values come *first*! Values lead to vision, which leads to mission accomplished.

Trike on!

6. Traditions Are Not Honored or Remembered

Coaching Character Through Time-Honored Traditions

Traditions, which span across various times and cultures in our history, often serve a purpose. Their essence? Through stories, legends, and various practices, traditions coach future generations by passing down wisdom and knowledge. Sometimes, the meanings embedded in traditions can fade with time, like a whispered secret losing its accuracy as it's conveyed through the chain of mouths.

In days gone by, people coached future generations on traditions to continue the rich heritage and culture being handed down. However, as time has evolved, we are losing our connection to our past history and the traditions that helped coach us in our cultures and society to bring us to the technologically mature world and cultures we live in today.

Not communicating and coaching these traditions can be dangerous. It can fracture our society, culture, communities, and families, and it can cause people to lose the inherent satisfaction of being connected to others in life.

So, coaching character goes much deeper than simply coaching an individual. Coaching character has much deeper and far-reaching implications in coaching our families, our communities, our societies, and our nation. Coaching character has a direct correlation to our health, wealth, and success of our future.

In my first book, *The Tricycle Effect* (in chapter 18), I explain the marriage ceremony and tradition and discuss with the reader a tradition we are all familiar with: the marriage or wedding ceremony.

My goal was to focus on how the marriage ceremony is steeped in tradition from hundreds of years ago, yet few people know why it is enacted the way it is. Even people hired to manage the ceremony and lead the rehearsal process may not know why certain things happen during the ceremony.

Take, for instance, the simple act of understanding which side of the father the bride walks on as they head down the aisle together. Because the marriage ceremony is steeped in character values, the bride should walk down the aisle on the right-hand side of her father.

I wrote about the marriage tradition because it embodies deep, rich character values. The ceremony is not just going through the technical motions of getting married. It is meant to communicate something much deeper about character skills with honor and respect as the bride and groom take their vows and everyone attending recognizes the oath that each person vows to one another.

Let's review the ceremony tradition and delve a bit into history and biblical contexts to unravel this tradition's mystery. The Bible, a several-thousand-year-old document, tells us that after Christ's resurrection, Christ was seated at the right hand of God, the Father, symbolizing a place of honor, respect, and even protection.

Military traditions echo a similar sentiment. Soldiers hold weapons in their right hands, signaling that those on their right are in a place of honor, respect, trust, and protection as they are not threatened by the weapon.

This military tradition plays a profound role in the wedding ceremony. The bride, since her birth, has been under her father's metaphorical umbrella of honor, respect, trust, and protection. It's not about subjugation—it's about honor, respect, and protection. The image of God placing Christ at His right hand is paralleled in the tradition that the bride should walk down the aisle on her father's right side, showing he has always been and is still putting his daughter in the position of honor, respect, trust, and protection.

Upon reaching the end of the aisle, the father kisses the bride and takes his seat on the left-hand side of the congregation. Notice that he does not have to cross over the aisle to get to the mother of the bride. The bride then moves to the groom, and initially stands to the groom's left. After they are pronounced husband and wife, and the couple turns around to face the audience, the bride is now on the groom's right side, again signifying that the groom has replaced the father and now holds the position of providing honor, respect, trust, and protection to the bride. He has literally succeeded the father and will continue to hold the bride in a position of honor, respect, trust, and protection.

Just imagine if all traditions were used to coach our younger generations in this meaningful and thoughtful way. Perhaps, the understanding and application of such profound traditions would lead to less divorce and domestic violence. It might once again offer spectators at the wedding ceremony a tangible representation of the couple's commitment to honoring, respecting, trusting, and protecting each other throughout their life journeys together.

Let me give you a great example of how this tradition actually extends to other areas of life that I practice even today at gymnastics meets. You can watch me do this at any meet with my gymnasts. After warm-ups, before a gymnastics meet starts, there is generally a march in or introduction of the teams and judges. During that time, the teams line up at their first event in a single line. Then the national anthem is played. Before the national anthem begins, I always walk up to my gymnasts, who again are all in a line for introductions, and stand on the far left side, right in line with them. We all put our right hands over the left sides of our hearts. I stand on their left side, so they are to my right. That way, as the gym dad, I have all my daughters to my right in the position of honor, respect, trust, and protection.

Coach Dane and his little gymnast to his right getting ready to compete Floor Exercise.

The real reason I do this is to coach my gym daughters on a tradition that they may have never heard or experienced before but may provide them with a meaningful tradition in their future marriages with their mates, families, and generations to come.

So, I invite you to reflect and ask yourself: Which traditions have been handed down to you in your family? What traditions may have slipped through your fingers? Which cultural practices within your family could you revive, investing in their meanings and ensuring that such understanding is imparted upon your family or culture? How can you be coaching tradition for yourself and those around you to add value and make a difference in their lives?

In conclusion, many barriers can prevent individuals from being coach-able, including fear of failure, resistance to change, lack of self-awareness, lack of accountability, and a fixed mindset. Overcoming these barriers requires developing a growth mindset, being open to feedback, and being willing to take calculated risks. By developing coach-ability, individuals can achieve greater personal and professional success.

Just like the motto they live by at West Point, "Duty, Honor, Country."...trike on!

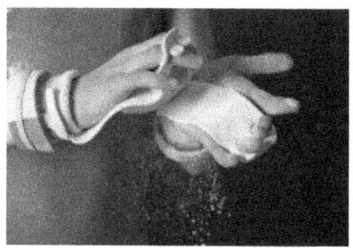

Chalk Talk Coaching Tip

In this chapter, "Barriers to Coach-Ability," I identify fear of failure, resistance to change, lack of self-awareness, lack of accountability, and a fixed mindset as critical barriers to becoming coach-able. Overcoming these barriers is essential for personal and professional growth and requires intentional effort to develop a growth mindset, where mistakes become opportunities for learning, and success and failure are treated with the same resilience.

- **Promise of solution:** Acknowledging that failure is a natural and valuable part of the learning process empowers individuals to engage with challenges more intelligently and with resilience, promoting continual improvement and mastery.

- **Suggested action step**: Start reframing your approach to failure by setting a weekly experimentation goal, where you deliberately step outside of your comfort zone in a small but significant way. After each attempt, whether it ends in success or failure, document what you learned and how this new insight can influence your future actions.

This practice will help cultivate a growth mindset where failure is not a setback but an informative step forward. In addition, I also recommend that you download my "Honor Code" and use it to help you navigate your true north on your moral compass. You can download it at https://www.lmdc.us/links/free-resources.

The Tricycle Effect Free Resources

Workbook for Coach-Ability, Chapter 7

Barriers to Coach-Ability

Fill-in-the-Blanks

1. Fear of failure is one of the most common barriers to coach-ability, and overcoming it requires being intentional and developing a _____ mindset.

2. When we discuss traditions and their importance in coaching character, we understand that these practices are not just about going through the motions, but they are meant to communicate deeper values of _____, _____, _____, and _____.

3. Overcoming resistance to change can be a significant barrier to coach-ability, and it requires developing a growth mindset, being open to new _____, and being willing to take calculated _____.

Reflective Questions

1. Reflect on a time when fear of failure held you back from taking action. What were the circumstances, and how might you approach a similar situation differently now, based on the insights from this chapter?

2. Consider a time when you experienced resistance to change. How did this affect your ability to grow and adapt, and what strategies could you implement to overcome such resistance in the future?

3. Recall an experience where a lack of self-awareness or accountability in yourself or others led to a missed opportunity or challenge. How did this affect the situation, and what steps can you take to foster greater self-awareness and accountability moving forward?

Summary of Chapter 7 Workbook

Chapter 7 of *Coach-ability* illuminates the common barriers that hinder our path to becoming coach-able: the fear of failure, resistance to change, lack of self-awareness, lack of accountability, and having a fixed mindset. The chapter stresses that recognizing and confronting these obstacles is crucial for growth in personal and professional realms. A growth mindset, characterized by embracing challenges and seeing mistakes as learning opportunities, is advocated as a remedy for these barriers.

Traditions, too, play a significant role in character coaching, emphasizing the importance of values such as honor, respect, and trust. This chapter calls for a reflective and proactive approach to self-coaching, where overcoming the barriers to coach-ability leads to a journey of continual learning and self-improvement. It is a reminder that through resilience, adaptability, and a commitment to character-first leadership, we can transform obstacles into stepping-stones for success and significance.

CHAPTER 8

How to Overcome Barriers to Coach-Ability

Experience isn't the best teacher; evaluated experience is. — John C. Maxwell[50]

IN THE PREVIOUS CHAPTER, we discussed the common barriers to coach-ability. In this chapter, we will explore how to overcome these barriers, including adopting self-reflection and awareness, seeking support and guidance, challenging limiting beliefs, embracing a growth mindset, and taking small steps toward change.

1. Self-Reflection and Awareness

Self-reflection and awareness are essential for overcoming barriers to coach-ability. By reflecting on your behaviors and actions, individuals can identify areas for improvement and develop self-awareness. Developing self-awareness requires being open to feedback, asking for help, and being willing to learn and grow.

> **Challenge/Problem statement:** Overcoming limiting beliefs and embracing a growth mindset is essential, since without it individuals may stagnate, missing opportunities for development and success.

While in the military, I was part of what is called RED Team. The RED Team is responsible for building the war scenario, throwing quarter-sized sticks of dynamite and smoke grenades, and simulation-based injuries with people to stage scenarios that are as real as possible.

During the war-time exercise scenarios, we would hand scenario cards to different people in the "play area" and then actively observe their actions or inactions to evaluate their performance. Most of the time, people did pretty well, but there were occasions when the people responding to the scenario failed the evaluation. What's interesting is that many times the people who failed were also the people who did not like to receive any kind of feedback, even if it was constructive. Rather than embracing the evaluation feedback and making appropriate changes or asking for help, they would make excuses. Or worse, at times, they'd get so hotheaded that they would strike out at someone.

The exercise scenarios were generally so realistic that the war games themselves, played continuously over three days, would drive people into intense emotional states. I noticed that the best players were the ones who took feedback well, no matter how big of a mistake they had made. They simply learned from their mistake, quickly adjusted to make the changes, and were then eager to show they learned from their mistakes. After the exercises, they could not wait to get a chance to redeem themselves in the next war game.

Normally, after very intensive exercises that were played for 72 hours or longer, there was always what we called a debrief, where each team member explained what they did well, where they could improve, and what their goals were the next time.

The most interesting part of the debrief was that rank did not matter. As a first lieutenant, I had to debrief about 100 people on the mistakes a security police commander and his squadron had made in IT authentication. There was a two-star general in the audience listening to the debrief, and it was my job to explain how this commander failed a major portion of the exercise.

The commander was not happy that I did that, but he took the advice, made the changes, and trained his squadron. After the next exercise, I was able to report that they did not break policies on IT authentication and their squadron got an outstanding rating.

Takeaways from This Lesson

1. No matter rank, position or authority, *debriefs* are very important. I was even told once that pilots wear their rank attached their flight suits with Velcro so that they can easily take their rank off before going into combat *but also during the debrief*. If a general was on a mission as a pilot, he had to attend the debrief after the mission like all the other pilots. If the general went into the debrief with his rank on, there might be the possibility that a lower-ranking officer could feel intimidated and not want to provide honest feedback if they were the

one who saw the general screw up. This is especially true if someone did not get the right feedback, and without making appropriate changes, there is the potential that the error could put other pilots or team members at risk the next time. In the corporate world, leaders need to have this mental stance as well. This means that the pilots must be able to be humble and exhibit the *humility* spoke on the character skills wheel.

2. Being coach-able means being hungry to learn and grow. My best team members were always those who were hungry regardless of whether they were right or not. It was all about improving themselves for the betterment of the team. Even in our gym with our little athletes, I ask them from time to time if they are hungry. New athletes will think I am talking about food, but I am really trying to get them to be aware that they are not showing or exhibiting enough hunger to learn.

3. Another key character skill exhibited here is *empathy*. A friend of mine who is a general, and who has spoken with several other generals says that the number one skill that generals believe makes them successful is empathy. In the debrief, no one wants to be called out, but when they are, and everyone sooner or later is, then they can empathize with others, which makes them even more motivated to make changes, improve their performance, and move on!

4. The last thing that I believe is really important is *BLUF* (bottom line up front). Too often during debriefs, people want to water down the impact of decisions and may even choose to leave their biggest mistakes until the end. In the military, pilots like *clarity*. According to Carmine Gallo, "Clarity is at the heart of a mission brief. Clarity is achieved through the acronym BLUF. BLUF is a concise recap of the essential message, and it's always 'up front,' or at the beginning of a discussion."[51] It is absolutely essential that, for a debrief to be effective and result in real change that is meaningful, no one waters anything down, hides facts, or minimizes something simply because the effect or ramifications afterward were not critical this time. Brutal honesty with self can only be experienced by those leaders who understand that self-awareness is the key to having the willingness to ask for feedback, accept the feedback, make appropriate changes, and then learn and grow.

5. Stephen Covey wrote in his book *The Speed of Trust* that "we judge ourselves by our intentions and others by their actions."[52] Many times we do not see ourselves for who we really are in our actions. We see ourselves and judge ourselves by our intentions. If we could get used to having others in our personal and professional lives help us with feedback to see our true selves, how much more in life could we really accomplish? This is probably the number one reason why we all need coaches, not just for sports but for other areas as well, such as executive roles,

life, family, speaking, leadership, management, and many more. If you have not considered hiring a coach, I highly recommend it. A great coach can help you most by asking the right questions for you to learn your real self, increase your awareness of your strengths and weaknesses, and help you learn to grow to be more successful for yourself and more significant for others. Remember, based on the Tricycle Effect, success is adding value to ourselves, and significance is adding value to others. If we don't take time to self-reflect and become aware of our self-talk regarding our dreams, our purposes, our passions, there may not be enough insight for us to learn best.

> As Ken Blanchard says, "Feedback is the breakfast of champions."[4]

If you want to be a champion in any area of life, you need feedback to help you become better than you can become all by yourself. Coaches give you the feedback, and if you are hungry to feed yourself what the coaches provide you and make the changes necessary to accomplish the next step or goal you are striving for, then you will become a champion.

So, I encourage you to be a champion and get and stay hungry! Eat that feedback for breakfast!

2. Seeking Support and Guidance

Seeking support and guidance can help individuals overcome barriers to coach-ability. This can involve seeking feedback from a coach or mentor, attending training or development programs, or working with a therapist or counselor. By seeking support and guidance, individuals can develop new skills and strategies to overcome the barriers to coach-ability.

To seek support and guidance, we need to be humble. Humility is absolutely essential to being coach-able. And humility, or having humility, is, of course, a spoke on the character skill wheel in the Tricycle Effect.

Humility doesn't necessarily mean weakness. Many times, being humble means being courageous enough to ask others for help and being smart enough and intelligent enough to know when to ask for that help.

On one occasion, when I was what we call a butter bar lieutenant (a second lieutenant), I was ordered by a colonel to give a high-performance score to one of my sergeants. I had written a performance report and given the person a very low score on the performance report because that was the score they deserved. They truly had earned it. I had everything documented in what I wrote, too, so the score was justified.

I turned it in expecting that I was all done. However, not long after that, my colonel called me and said, "I don't want you to give this person such a low score, because I don't want this person to stay at our base. I want him to be able to move on, and if this report with the low-performance score gets to the next base, once they see that he has a low score, they will cancel his ability to go to the new base, and we'll be stuck with him."

As I learned, the only things that are transferred to the next base are the actual scores from performance reports. I let the colonel know that I was being honest, and in good conscience, I couldn't give that person a high score since I knew the truth of how he had actually performed.

I really struggled with that order and had no idea how I was going to obey it while remaining true to my conscience. I reached out to ask other officers on what to do. I also happened to go to a prayer breakfast at the base and brought up a prayer request for this very thing. Afterward, once we finished the breakfast and prayer, a colonel came up to me and said, "I think I can help you with that problem you are having."

"It's very simple," he said. "You give the sergeant a perfect score. Then you will have obeyed the order. Write nothing on the back of the performance report where you would normally explain and justify the score. So for the personnel center, when they send the score to the next base, they will see a perfect score. When he arrives at the next base and they look at his performance report and see that there's nothing written on the back, it will send them a strong message that he was a very poor performer. And you will have told everyone that he was a very poor performer and had poor performance, giving them a heads-up that they need to be careful about watching him, managing him, and so forth. That way you will have abided by the legal order to give him a high score in terms of a number while at the same time told the real story and truth that he was a poor performer. So you will have accomplished both things that you need."

And so that's what I did, and that person left our base. I never heard another thing after that. My colonel was happy. I was happy, and we accomplished what we needed to do. To be honest, if I hadn't been humble in asking for help, I probably wouldn't have gotten that help. There have been many times in my career where I humbled myself and went and told someone I didn't know the answer. I needed their help. Or I needed them to help me brainstorm because I knew they had a background with that particular expertise. Maybe I just flat-out didn't know what to do. I even needed someone to help me brainstorm where to get started.

But all of that hinged on being humble. In other words, being humble, and humility, is one of the spokes on the front character skill wheel in the Tricycle Effect.

Most leaders in charge of a company or organization believe they need to know all the answers because they are the leader. That could not be further from the truth. People respect others who are genuine and authentic. Everyone knows that nobody knows everything, so why put on that fakery?

Even in my university classes, I told the students I was not perfect at the beginning of the semester and apologized, half-heartedly, for being a human. I told them that I was not perfect and was sorry to disappoint them if they were looking for an instructor who knew all the answers. I also told them that if I did not know the answers, that I would just say that I did not know and would find out and get an answer back to them later.

Believe it or not, I never felt less of a teacher or coach for setting that kind of expectation in the teaching environment. I actually felt empowered, which may seem strange, but I did not have something to hide, like knowing all the answers, and therefore, I could just be myself and be authentic and genuine. I really think the students appreciated that.

That is also why I told them they could call me Mr. Deutsch or professor, but I preferred being called Coach, and that is what most of them call me even today when we connect on LinkedIn and other social media channels.

Being humble allows us to be coached successfully. The colonel who coached me to be able to accomplish what I was ordered to do but yet do what was in my heart and conscience, along with my integrity, had the answer. I was so grateful to him.

He gave me a key to understanding integrity by serving me with a solution to something that appeared to have no resolution. He knew what I needed to do, and through his wisdom and experience, he gave me the opportunity to stay honest and true to myself with my moral compass. So there you go, team—being coach-able is more fun when you're humble, authentic, genuine, and true to self.

Stay humble and trike on!

3. Challenging Limiting Beliefs

Challenging limiting beliefs is essential for overcoming barriers to coach-ability. Many barriers to coach-ability are rooted in limiting beliefs, such as a fear of failure, a fixed mindset, or even a concept called impostor syndrome. By challenging these beliefs and adopting a growth mindset, individuals can learn to embrace challenges and setbacks as opportunities for learning and growth.

Harnessing the Power of Self-Talk and Coaching in Gymnastics

In our journey through coach-ability, we discover that sometimes the most pivotal coaching doesn't come from an external source but from within us—our self-talk. We have already talked about self-talk quite a bit, but it is so important that I want to emphasize it from a different perspective and dig a little deeper.

Coaching often comes from external figures, but the most crucial coaching, at times, springs from our own inner dialogue where we coach ourselves through self-talk. The way we converse with ourselves, how we structure our internal environment, and how we frame our perceptions—be it considering hazards, challenges, or opportunities—all can play a critical role in laying out our path in life. If our self-talk isn't positive, we might coach ourselves out of opportunities. This is often referred to as self-sabotage or negative self-talk. But if we view this self-dialogue more as self-coaching, it just might alter our response to this internal conversation.

For example, I've worked with many gymnasts over the years whose negative self-talk hindered their performance. Phrases like *I can't do it* or *it's too hard for me* or *I might as well stop trying* were common. That kind of self-talk gets them stuck, and they don't know a way forward, nor will they find one. In such instances, I always emphasized the power of the word *yet*—telling them to finish their thoughts with *I can't do it...yet*. In other words, they need to finish their English sentences. This small addition transforms their self-coaching, enabling their minds to envision future success and establish attainable goals. They essentially become "unstuck."

One gymnast, let's call her Ashley, struggled with a bar routine skill—translating from a cast to a handstand and swinging under the bar and back up to another handstand, known as a free hip handstand. These individual skills are sometimes called tricks. Physically, she was more than capable. As a level-eight gymnast, she was advanced enough and actually could do advanced skills. In gymnastics, there are 10 levels of advancement and then the elite gymnasts we all see on television and in the Olympics. So she was pretty advanced. However, it wasn't the physical prowess or skill that held her back but her mental block—her belief of *I can't get this* and her internal narration of failure impeded her progress. She was stuck. Often, we do not hear this self-talk, as it is quietly murmured within your mind, just like in her case. It was her self-talk that kept her from being successful in doing the skill or trick.

On one occasion, she executed a near-perfect free hip handstand with minimal gymnastics spotting, or help from me. Trying to boost her confidence, I pointed out that she had essentially done it by herself. Ashley's internal coach (the voice in her head), however, was not convinced. I urged her to believe she could do it by telling herself *I can do this!* She responded, "That would be a lie."

In effect, she may have actually been experiencing what is called impostor syndrome. People want to set goals for themselves, and they really do want to be successful, but they just can't bring themselves to believe or even think they could actually be like others they respect and look up to—people who have been or are already successful doing the same thing they want to be or are doing. Impostor syndrome is a very debilitating type of self-talk, and an inner-coach thought pattern that can hold you back and keep you from accomplishing your goals. This may also be the reason so many people do not reach their full potential in whatever endeavor they are working toward in life. A growth mindset may very well be the cure needed to get yourself unstuck from time to time. As reported by NeuroLeadership Institute, impostor syndrome "becomes a self-fulfilling prophecy in that you no longer benefit from potential learning opportunities." In this article, it states that a growth mindset may be the cure. "The more you believe your abilities are malleable, the more likely you are to focus on developing them, knowing you have the potential to do so."[54]

This gymnast thought acknowledging her ability to do the skill before fully believing she could do it would be dishonest to herself. In her mind, that meant she was actually telling a lie to herself. Your internal coaching, how you encourage or discourage yourself and frame each moment as potential opportunities or risks worth taking, holds immeasurable weight. Weeks later, Ashley was performing the skill independently, yet it took considerable time before she would admit, even to herself, "I can do this. This is my skill. I am not an impostor. I own this trick."

Imagine if she coached herself positively earlier on. She might have mastered the skill weeks before because she was, technically, already executing it on her own. It's vital to visualize, in our mind's eye, owning a skill or completing a task before it becomes reality. Thus, self-coaching might just be the most crucial skill set we need before we seek to coach others. While positive self-talk propels us forward, it's not enough on its own. Action must follow. Yet, with positive coaching from within and encouragement from teammates and coaches alike, achievements become attainable. Even the impossible many times becomes possible.

So, remember to stay coach-able in your self-talk. Control the inner coach, and you will have a better handle on controlling the outcome to be more successful for yourself and be more significant for others.

Trike on!

4. Embracing a Growth Mindset — Belief in Yourself

Just like Ashley overcoming negative self-talk, we know that embracing a growth mindset is critical for overcoming barriers to coach-ability. A growth mindset is a belief that abilities can be developed through hard work and dedication. Individuals with a growth mindset are more open to feedback, willing to try new things, and persistent in the face of setbacks.

Sometimes organizations have teams, like sports teams, that work together to come up with the next best technology or a solution to a really tough problem. Those teams are sometimes called masterminds. In a mastermind, the cumulative power of all brains together is much greater than any one brain alone, and that is why they call these teams masterminds.

Masterminds exist in the business world just as they do with sports teams. This same concept even applies to family life as well. When family members and teammates are encouraging you, sometimes you can do things you never dreamed of doing.

A great example of this is the creation of the first computer and mouse. Do you know who invented the first computer with a graphical user interface (GUI) where there were images (graphics) on the computer screen and a mouse to click on the images? It was not Microsoft, and it was not Apple. It was Xerox. Xerox at the Palo Alto Research Center invented the first GUI and mouse.[55] They created a team and put this group of people together in a "skunkworks" group.[56] Generally, skunkworks teams were secretive and consisted of many of the brightest and best minds in a company assembled with a task to come up with something new that would solve an identified problem. So, Xerox did just that. Someone wanted to find out what the next generation of computer technology would look like. The Xerox skunkworks team designed a computer with a GUI and mouse, which had not been done before.

In this case, Xerox did exactly what teams are designed to do: perform better than any one person can perform all by themselves. They had no holds barred and came up with a concept no one had thought of.

However, today, Xerox does not make personal computers and has never really gotten into the business of making personal computers. Shortly after showcasing their new computer GUI product, Xerox discontinued their work on computer development. Basically, they threw the idea away because someone did not believe there would be a customer demand for it. Boy, were they wrong! Two entities did, however, attend the showcase and picked up where Xerox left off—the founders of Microsoft and Apple. Today, Microsoft and Apple are what they have become, thanks to Xerox. Unfortunately, Xerox did not recognize the gold mine they'd discovered and never took advantage of their skunkworks team's discovery and genius. Today, Xerox is best known for its printers and copiers.

Sometimes, we might have the answer but cut it short because we don't see the need or understand the demand for it. Again, this is another reason to have a coach or team to help give us a 360-degree view of things and maybe see things we don't. We sure don't want to miss an opportunity or possibility for growth.

At whatever stage in life you are at now, you might be able to look back and realize that your team or family helped you in a way that you could not have done on your own. You might even ask yourself, How did I do that? It was almost as if you were superhuman. And you were because you had more people behind you who were rooting for you and helping to encourage you. That is the power of a growth mindset in teamwork!

5. Taking Small Steps Toward Change

Taking small steps toward change is essential for overcoming barriers to coach-ability. Rather than trying to make significant changes all at once, individuals can start by taking small steps toward self-improvement. This can involve setting achievable goals, seeking feedback, and practicing new skills in a safe and supportive environment.

Taking small steps toward change happens almost every day in our gymnastics training center, especially when the athletes are hungry to learn a new skill that seems fun and exciting. When it's their idea, it is most likely even more exciting. They embrace that change and work toward the goal.

However, when it's the coach who wants them to learn a new skill or drill that is totally new that they have never heard of or seen, then that could be an entirely different situation. If I wanted my gymnasts, for instance, to tumble up onto stacked landing mats, they would probably give me some pushback right away.

If I don't tell them the complete end game or goal of the drill at the beginning and simply start them with just one small mat, they are most likely going to just go along with what I am instructing or coaching. So, maybe I start with a four-inch mat.

With such a small incremental step from what they are used to, they're probably not going to say anything. If I told them we're going to do a four-inch mat, and we're going to build up to four feet, they're probably going to give me pushback even before we start with the four-inch mat. So, sometimes it's best not to even say what the ultimate change or goal will be with the skill or drill. We just play with each small step as we go along.

With the four-inch mat we might be able to just say, "Hey, everybody made it on the four-inch mat! How about we add another four-inch mat?"

In that case, I'm just giving them an opportunity to be able to see that they're invested in the decision-making and adding to the skill, as they now have become comfortable with being able to do it successfully. Now we can move on, and it is logical to add something else. The gap between a four-inch mat and four feet of stacked mats becomes less daunting and more believable. That method of easing into change works very well when you can simply break steps to the goal down into small increments.

However, there are other times when, at some point, you have to actually complete the skill. For instance, you might have to salto (somersault in the air), or you might have to actually twist, and you can only do small changes and repeat those skills up to a certain point before attempting the whole skill. It's a little bit different, but the idea is the same. The key is to make as small a change as possible, even when we're twisting, for instance.

Brainstorming how to construct those small steps takes a lot of thought and strategy building. If I want my athletes to work on twisting, and they can do a layout (somersault in the air with a straight body), how would I get them to start twisting so they are not against that idea but are more willing to try something new? Well, I could actually make it a game. So, I might have the kids work to twist around a clock. If they're standing in one space, I tell them to imagine a clock underneath their feet where, on each attempt, they will try to twist from the 12:00 position to 1:00, and then 2:00, and then 3:00, 4:00, 5:00, and finally the 6:00 position for a half twist before they land. With small steps like this, we then can watch for any fears or bad habits that might start to happen. We can even show them and prove to them that they're not even twisting upside down at all before they land to make that twist.

So, we can minimize the fear factor by removing the idea of the gymnasts being upside down at all. Playing a little game with the clock sometimes allows small incremental steps to take the edge off abrupt changes—especially changes that were unknown earlier, which will ease gymnasts' minds and help them to avoid anxiety.

Take a look at this gymnast who is doing her first ever double back salto between uneven bars. I am not even spotting. I am taking the video from the side. We have done so many small little incremental steps that she can do this skill perfectly. Notice the stuck dismount! Again, this was her first ever double back between the uneven bars. Amazing accomplishments if we just take the small steps and play.

Level 9 gymnast - first double-back dismount on bars and without any Coach Spotting

So, small changes in sports are easy to understand, but small changes in business are just as important or even more so. I used this same technique to get my team in the U.S. Air Force to want to play war games in preparation for war in the Middle East.

Before we started, no one wanted to participate, even though they had just failed their operational readiness inspection. You would think that because we are military and preparing for war is what we do, everyone would be on board with that idea. As it turns out, not so much.

Change is inevitable, and as I said, you would think military people would just know that intuitively somehow, but remember they are human becomings first and foremost. So, even they needed to be coached into learning and doing new things.

Once we made our training into smaller, challenging, and fun group exercises, everyone wanted to play, and we began to improve. Buy-in was a huge part of taking small steps and creating change.

An example in business might be that one day the CEO walks into the business conference room and announces the company is going to add this new item or this product or this service, but yet they haven't briefed the change to the team or even given a heads-up to the team to find out what they think about it.

The normal reaction? Immediate pushback. Of course humans don't like change, especially change that does not involve their decision-making or buy-in. Remember that for your team to be coach-able, you need to prepare them to be coach-able. If you're going to actually make a change in an organization, the best practice is to do it slowly and methodically, almost as if it had its own strategy. This is similar to when we break these gymnastics skills down into small increments to learn twisting and back tumbling and skills like that. It's no different in business.

Remember that we are just big kids. By breaking change down into small steps or game strategies, you are more likely to get buy-in and be more successful in implementing change. Slow and steady wins the race, and I like to say small changes create big wins. Justin Thomas Miller calls this the butterfly effect and likes to say, "Small changes lead to big progress."[57]

And so it is in coaching yourself. Give yourself room to grow in your head by breaking down the seemingly impossible and building it up gradually through your self-talk and self-coaching, and you will find that nothing is impossible.

You can do it, my friend!

Trike on!

6. The Power of Body Position

The Transformative Power of a Smile

Body positions that we take or pose in are a direct reflection of what we are coaching ourselves, or saying to ourselves in our minds with our self-talk.

I am dedicating this chapter to the simple yet profound impact of a *smile*. Yes, even a smile is a body position, though most people would not think of it that way. But facial expressions are a part of our body talk.

I recently watched a TED Talk titled "The Hidden Power of Smiling," delivered by Ron Gutman[58] and shared by my mentor, Lee Ellis. The talk delved into how a smile, a mere curving of the lips, can pivotally shift your attitude and perspective.

In the gymnastics coaching realm, I emphasize not only the potency of visualizing routines or harnessing the might of self-talk but also the substantial influence of body language in self-coaching. This is applicable not just within the confines of the gym but stretches into every avenue of their lives, whether grappling with academic struggles, navigating through relationships, or managing other external stressors.

Here's a key concept I call the power position, which I introduce to my gymnasts, even the youngest ones aged five, six, or seven. You can use this too. It works even if you are a grown-up kid.

This involves confidently placing your hands on your hips, thumbs pointing backward, and fingers forward. This stance isn't merely a physical pose but an embodiment of internal empowerment. It reassures them that failure isn't a detriment but rather an insightful stepping-stone toward new beginnings.

Interestingly, everyone's paths to mastering a skill varies. Some may grasp it within a few attempts, while others may require hundreds of relentless tries. But regardless of the duration and intensity of the journey, if I guide them to channel their self-talk through body language, then they use what I call the power position. They can expedite their skill progression and even shorten their journeys to becoming really good gymnasts.

When gymnasts first begin their gymnastics career with us, they don't feel comfortable putting their hands on their hips. That is because they are not confident, and having your hands on your hips in a position of confidence communicates to yourself something different from what your self-talk is telling you. I just keep reminding them to keep their hands on their hips while waiting for their turn. In other words, stand in the power position.

It is amazing the transformation that happens. These little gymnasts who once were not confident are now, over time, comfortably confident in their environment and eager to take on new challenges, even if they don't know how to do them yet.

In instances of self-doubt, body position gives a gymnast away, because their body is visibly communicating with themselves and those around them through "fig leaf" hand positions or crossed arms, which show some level of fear, concern, or lack of confidence. I again gently instructed the gymnast to assume the power position.

Although initially reluctant, as their emotional state may not align with this display of strength, the physical act of adopting a powerful stance or position with their body informs their brain and compels it to match the confidence exhibited by their body. This is a critical realization: our body language can indeed lead us first and coach us to success!

Circling back to the principle of the smile, I want to share a personal strategy. On nights when my mind is engulfed in a tumultuous sea of thoughts, anxieties, and fears (and we all experience times like this, akin to a gymnast who feels defeated after numerous unsuccessful skill attempts), I've found a potent power position, even while lying in bed. Even though the conventional power position is impractical in a prone state, one can activate a powerful mental stance of relaxation through facial expression alone.

My gymnasts learn that a genuine power position encompasses not just their hands on hips but also a confident, assuring facial expression. When entangled in nocturnal worries when attempting to go to sleep, try this: Lie flat on your back, remove the pillow from under your head, allow your hands to rest by your side, relax, breathe slowly, then with your gaze directed toward the ceiling (yes, even in the dark), simply smile. Hold that smile longer than a few seconds, and soon, you'll find yourself waking up and greeting the morning, refreshed and ready to tackle the day ahead.

Our minds continue to work through issues even as we sleep, often providing solutions, or at least relief, from our concerns. Smiling before drifting off invites a positive, solution-oriented mindset to permeate our sleep, allowing us to wake up with resolved worries and a fresh perspective on problems.

So, my friend, in the spirit of coach-ability and trikin' on, I encourage you to smile—both in wakefulness and sleep—paving your way toward success, and transforming concerns into triumphs.

In conclusion, developing coach-ability requires overcoming the common barriers that can prevent individuals from being coach-able. Self-reflection and awareness, seeking support and guidance, challenging limiting beliefs, embracing a growth mindset, and taking small steps toward change can all help individuals overcome these barriers and achieve greater personal and professional success. By developing coach-ability, individuals can unlock their full potential and achieve their goals.

Trike on and smile!

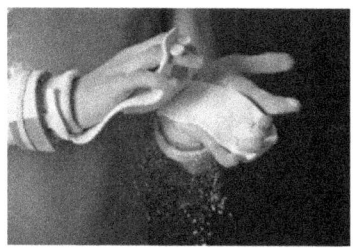

Chalk Talk Coaching Tip

In chapter 8, "How to Overcome Barriers to Coach-Ability," overcoming the barriers to coach-ability involves a blend of embracing self-reflection, seeking guidance, challenging limiting beliefs, and putting forth gradual, persistent effort. Embracing a growth mindset and actionable feedback, regardless of rank or status, equips individuals with the humility and adaptability needed to learn from experiences and develop the resilience essential for personal and professional advancement.

- **Promise of solution:** Recognizing and challenging limiting beliefs open the door to growth, fostering a mindset that welcomes continual learning and the ability to convert setbacks into progress.

- **Suggested action step**: Start journaling your daily experiences with a focus on moments where you feel limited by your beliefs. For each entry, write down the belief, question its validity, and replace it with an affirmative statement that reflects a growth mindset. This practice can help to reinforce the concept that abilities and intelligence can develop with effort and persistence, encouraging a more adaptable and proactive approach to personal and professional growth.

Workbook for Coach-Ability, Chapter 8
How to Overcome Barriers to Coach-Ability

Fill-in-the-Blanks

1. By reflecting on their behaviors and actions, individuals can identify areas for improvement and develop _____.

2. The RED Team is responsible for building the war scenario, throwing quarter sticks of dynamite and smoke grenades, as well as simulation-based injuries with people to stage scenarios that are as _____ as possible.

3. No matter the rank, position, or authority, _____ are very important for growth and learning from experiences.

Reflective Questions

1. Think about a time when you received feedback that was hard to accept. How did you handle the situation, and

what could you have done differently to use that feedback as a tool for growth?

2. Reflect on a belief about yourself that you now recognize as limiting. How did you come to realize this, and what steps have you taken to challenge and change that belief?

3. Consider the role of humility in seeking support and guidance. Can you share a personal experience where admitting you didn't have all the answers led to growth or learning?

Summary of Chapter 8 Workbook

Chapter 8 encourages a proactive approach to overcoming barriers to coach-ability. The chapter emphasizes the importance of self-reflection and awareness as foundational tools for identifying areas for growth. It highlights the necessity of being open to feedback, the value of seeking support, and the significance of challenging limiting beliefs. Embracing a growth mindset is portrayed not just as a beneficial trait but a critical one for personal development and success. Taking small steps toward change, engaging in debriefs to learn from both successes and failures, and the role of humility in learning are underlined as crucial for continual improvement. Through intentional effort and support, individuals can move past barriers and cultivate an environment ripe for growth and excellence. The chapter calls on readers to embrace the iterative process of self-coaching, reinforcing that with determination and the right mindset, barriers to coach-ability can be transformed into stepping-stones toward becoming better leaders and individuals.

Chapter 9
Coach-Ability in Personal Life

Coach-ability is not just essential for professional success, but it can also positively affect personal life. In this chapter, we will explore how coach-ability can lead to personal growth and self-improvement, as well as improved relationships and communication with others.

> **Challenge/Problem statement:** Fostering personal growth and maintaining enriching relationships can be hindered by a lack of coach-ability and resistance to introspection and change.

1. Personal Growth and Self-Improvement

Coach-ability can lead to personal growth and self-improvement by helping individuals identify their strengths and weaknesses, set goals, and develop new skills and strategies. Being open to feedback and constructive criticism can help individuals gain self-awareness and make positive changes to their behaviors and actions. Developing a growth mindset can also help individuals overcome obstacles and setbacks to achieve their goals.

I know I touched on it earlier, but I want to emphasize it again: we can learn from others and our experiences in any situation.

When we first opened our gym, we actually had a school bus that we drove from daycare to daycare to allow preschool children the opportunity to get outside for some physical activity an hour each week. We took all the seats in the bus out and we laid down foam and carpet with all the miniature gymnastics equipment just like we had in our big gym. We called our gym bus Jumpin' Gym-Mini, kind of a takeoff of Jiminy Cricket in the Disney movie *Pinocchio*.

Remember that Jiminy Cricket was the one who said, "Always let your conscience be your guide."[59]

Well, Jumpin' Gym-Mini wasn't a cricket, but he was a kangaroo, and of course, kangaroos jump, so the name matched the character. Each day of the week, I would drive on a tour of cities with daycares. On Monday, I might go east to three or four cities and serve daycares in each city in that direction. Each day of the week was the same. Every daycare had Jumpin' Gym-Mini buttons they would put on the kids on the day Gym-Mini came to their daycare to exercise and play with them. The bus concept was before its time and well before characters like Barney.

I digress a bit, but I want to emphasize that sometimes preparing the environment helps to coach others and, in turn, build stronger and more trusting relationships with those people and children as well.

Remember Art Linkletter's show *Kids Say the Darndest Things?* Sometimes those kids would say something and answer honestly, many times resulting in adults learning something they did not know before. Well, each time I took Gym-Mini out to visit the children, I would honestly learn as much from the kids as I was teaching them.

For instance, I may have thought that I gave clear instructions, but the kids would interpret exactly what I said and do that instead of what I really wanted. An example might be when they were on the top of a bar. Most preschoolers would put their tummies on the bar while still holding onto the bar. But their arms were bent, so I would tell them, "Straighten your arms." Well, *straighten your arms* for preschoolers means letting go of the bar and straightening your arms. Not safe, but they followed my instructions exactly.

So, I learned to demonstrate a lot more and talk in much slower kid language by thinking like them and wondering how they would respond to my instructions. Kids not only say the darndest things, but they also do the darndest things. We could all probably benefit from understanding that.

I sometimes tell people that I learned more from my preschool gymnastics students than from anyone else because they made things simple and did things opposite of what I wanted. They made mistakes, failed in funny ways, and lots more. And when they did, many times I would say to myself, Oh my! That is a great leadup for my advanced gymnasts.

Who knew that a preschooler could teach a gymnastics coach how to coach higher-level gymnasts? Sometimes the answers to some of life's toughest questions come from the least expected places—out of the mouths of babes. Keep it simple! Life is short, make it fun!

Trike on!

2. Improved Relationships and Communication

Coach-ability can also lead to improved relationships and communication with others. By being open to feedback and constructive criticism, individuals can improve their ability to listen actively and communicate effectively. Individuals who are coach-able are more likely to seek out the perspectives and opinions of others, which can help build trust and respect. Being coach-able can also help individuals take responsibility for their actions and be accountable for their behavior, which can improve relationships and communication.

Story About Visualization, Self-Coaching, and Achievement in Life, Sports, and Business

Understanding the profound impact of a positive mindset and belief system on our self-coaching abilities can sometimes be a complex journey. Let's explore this concept through a really meaningful illustration, initially touched upon in my first book.

My mother introduced me to *Psycho-Cybernetics* by Dr. Maxwell Maltz in seventh grade.[60] This book illuminated my understanding of self-talk and personal coaching. Even as a seventh grader, I could understand that book written by a doctor. He kept the cookies on the bottom shelf. And, boy, did I eat a lot of cookies!

My youthful adventures in wrestling, and later an AAU State Wrestling Championship win at 145 pounds in Minnesota, were not solely due to my technical wrestling prowess. I was a very good wrestler, no doubt about that. But my unshakable belief and visualization of winning each match before even stepping onto the mat became my secret weapons. Later in life, they also became my secret business weapons to success, both in the military as well as the corporate world!

Visualization and self-coaching have always held a pivotal role in my life, as well as in my coaching approach with gymnasts. There are two predominant visualization techniques I teach:

1. *Theater in the mind* occurs when you visualize actions on a mental screen. Visualization is more than a mental exercise. Gymnasts visualize themselves performing on a

screen they are watching, much like in a movie theater. Done correctly, with embedded emotions and sensory experiences, visualization can effectively build neural pathways in our brain, preparing us for the physical enactment of the task.

2. *In-body* is when the gymnast sees themself inside their body as if they are going along for the ride in their own body as they do tricks and routines. The more of the six senses they can create and experience in their mind's eye, and the more real they imagine those sensations, the more effective the in-body virtual training becomes. That means they lie down and visualize themselves going through each move in a routine, for instance. Before they start, they visualize standing in front of the bar ready to mount, hearing their teammates around them and smelling the chalk. Then once they jump to grab the bar, they feel the bar in their hands, their legs stiffen by tightening their muscles in their legs, then air whizzes by, and the bar is above their head, etc. Again, the more sensations they can feel while visualizing helps to make the virtual experience more effective.

Let me share a critical lesson regarding visualization from my coaching experience. A gymnast, when asked about her mental visualization technique, revealed that she visualized someone else performing instead of herself. I had never thought that one of my gymnasts might do that. I always instructed each of them to see themselves.

Somehow that got misinterpreted, and this was a pivotal misstep for her. Visualization must be a personal experience, picturing yourself in action to be effective.

Another crucial aspect is communication between the coach and the athlete about their visualization journey. Recognizing and addressing "black spots" in visualization, where the mental movie stops or breaks, are vital to working through mental blocks and enabling the physical execution of a skill or routine.

In my coaching journey, I've seen firsthand how powerful the brain is and how it can sometimes act as a barrier, even with the knowledge that the perceived danger or challenge is not real. With the emergence of virtual reality technologies, we've witnessed how the brain perceives virtual experiences as real, sometimes inhibiting physical actions due to the fear instilled by the virtual scenario. The brain is an astonishingly powerful organ, capable of feats far beyond our current understanding and technological advancements, even in the realm of AI.

To emphasize that concept, let me ask you if you have ever put on 3-D, virtual reality goggles. Maybe you haven't, but most people have by now these days. Even if I point out to you, before you put on your virtual reality headset, that the ground is flat in front of you and there is no drop-off in front of you at all, when the virtual reality headset presents you with an image of a cliff in front of you, and you are asked to step forward, your brain will not allow you to do that. To the brain, what is presented to it *is reality*!

The same is true with visualization. You cannot effectively visualize a trick or routine unless you can see yourself successfully completing it.

Reminder—my gymnastics coach said that each virtual routine you do properly and correctly in your mind is worth five physical routines. For instance, if I tell my gymnasts we have five physical routines to do tonight, they automatically know that after each routine, they must visualize it before they can go to the next station or chalk up for the next physical routine.

So, five physical plus five virtual, where one virtual equals five physical, means five physical plus 25 virtual equals 30 routines for the night.

But notice we have not physically beat up the body since we only did five total physical routines. We save the wear and tear on the gymnast's body and work much smarter rather than harder. And, when I say that, it takes a lot of focus and hard work to visualize an entire routine in any event in gymnastics. At first, it would seem fairly simple, but it is a lot harder than it looks (no pun intended).

> Integrate visualization and self-coaching into your practice regimen to harness the power of your mind in achieving goals and mastering tasks, whether it's delivering a speech or nailing a gymnastic routine.

Picture yourself from start to finish. Experience the sensations and emotions, and immerse yourself in the entirety of the action. It could be in the theater of your mind or in an in-body experience. Remember, for every meticulous virtual run-through, you're enhancing not just your mental preparedness but actually building neural pathways that facilitate physical execution.

In addition, you will attract all the right things into your life that will allow whatever you visualize to happen. Some people call this the law of attraction.

I believe in visualization, and I am a big believer in the law of attraction because I have seen it work in my own life for multiple roles:

- Wrestling champion
- Eagle Scout
- College graduate
- U.S. Air Force commissioned officer
- Cadet commander and communications site commander
- Chief of maintenance
- Coach
- Dad
- Husband
- Gymnastics coach
- Winner of various awards
- And many more

Visualization was the key to all of those accomplishments. Once I started visualizing the result of what I wanted, the law of attraction kicked in, and other people came to offer help or an actual job.

In your pursuit of life mastery, I encourage you to visualize, self-coach with affirmative and powerful self-talk, and immerse yourself in mental, virtual rehearsals. Engage in this practice and witness your capacities for learning and growth grow exponentially. And always remember, staying coach-able and being adaptable in your visualization and physical practices are keys to continual improvement and success.

Keep pedaling forward, stay coach-able, and trike on, team!

3. Prioritizing Values over Everything Else

According to John C. Maxwell in *There's No Such Thing as "Business" Ethics*, "Jim Collins, the author of *Built to Last* and *Good to Great*, has done extensive research into what makes companies highly successful. When he was asked what his research indicated about the importance of ethics in building a successful company, Collins replied, 'Our research points to one essential element in any successful company. Those that are the best have built a set of core values and lived by them.' "[61]

This speaks to companies, but it applies to individuals as well. I tell people all the time, "We *do not* have a corrupt government." I normally get some strange faces when I say that and even an objection once in a while. However, everyone in the audience generally agrees with me when I tell them, "We *do not* have a corrupt government, but we do have corrupt *people* in government." That means the individuals who make up the government are corrupt, or at the very least, they are not prioritizing character values in their lives.

If we don't prioritize character skill values and live a life by leading with character first, then we are on a path without direction or goals that are meaningful. Remember that the front wheel on the Tricycle Effect reflects all the character skills and values we should be embracing in life and leading ourselves with as well as our families and companies or organizations.

I really like the question that John C. Maxwell asks in chapter 1, titled "There is No Such Thing as Business Ethics, There is Just Ethics." In that book, he asks, "Whatever happened to business ethics?"[62] That is a great question, and John provides lots of evidence and rationale to explain why business ethics is in such a terrible state.

That brings the whole idea of ethics into a relatable topic that we can each identify with. Too many people today say things like *That's okay because it is just business.* That type of rationalization does not help us focus on character skill values at all or on helping those around us.

We should lead with character skill values and ask questions: "Is this kind? Is this trustworthy? Is this respectful?" Asking questions like those helps us to dial in character skill values into our lives, and thereby feel and sense more satisfaction, joy, and fulfillment in life.

I am afraid most people really don't know how to experience more satisfaction or joy or fulfillment in life. They conflate position, or more money, or more power, or more status as the key(s) to get there when in reality, it is only by living with character skill values that will bring us true happiness with real satisfaction, joy, and fulfillment in life.

We must coach ourselves in our personal lives to grow our character skills. Sadly, almost no one equates character values with skills. Let me ask you, "How do you become more respectful unless you practice being respectful?"

You could simply replace the word *respectful* with any character value such as trustworthy, fair, caring, responsible, loyal, empathetic, and more. You get the idea. Character values, if they are something you truly value, will become your priority, and you will work to improve them, practice them, and execute them in your personal life and your business life.

In conclusion, coach-ability is not just essential for professional success, but it can also positively affect personal life. By being open to feedback and constructive criticism, we can all achieve personal growth and self-improvement, as well as improve our relationships and communications with others. By developing coach-ability, individuals can unlock their full potential, achieve their goals, and make a positive impact in their personal and professional lives.

Stay coach-able! Trike on!

Chalk Talk Coaching Tip

Coach-ability enriches personal life by fostering personal growth and self-improvement. It allows individuals to identify their strengths and weaknesses, set meaningful goals, and develop strategies for self-enhancement. Moreover, it improves relationships and communication, as a coach-able person actively listens and effectively engages with others, building stronger, trust-based connections.

- **Promise of solution:** By embracing coach-ability, individuals can unlock pathways to self-improvement and foster deeper connections with others, leading to a more fulfilling and enriched life.

- **Suggested action step**: Commit to weekly reflection sessions where you ask for and document feedback from family and friends on specific behaviors, actively working on one area of improvement at a time. This process will nurture a growth mindset and enhance your relationships through better understanding and communication.

Workbook for Coach-Ability, Chapter 9
COACH-ABILITY IN PERSONAL LIFE

Fill-in-the-Blanks

1. Being open to _____ and constructive criticism can help individuals gain self-awareness and make positive changes to their behaviors and actions.

2. Coach-ability can lead to personal growth by helping individuals set _____ and develop new skills and strategies.

3. Developing a _____ mindset can help individuals overcome obstacles and setbacks and achieve their goals.

Reflective Questions

1. How have I applied coach-ability in my personal growth and self-improvement efforts, and what specific outcomes did I notice?

2. Can I recall a time when being coach-able led to an

improvement in my relationships or communication, and what were the changes I observed in myself and others?

3. Reflect on a situation where I resisted feedback. How could approaching it with a coach-able mindset have altered the outcome?

Summary of Chapter 9 Workbook

This chapter delves into how being coach-able is not just beneficial for your professional life but can also significantly enhance personal development. Embracing feedback and a growth mindset leads to a better understanding of your strengths and weaknesses, contributing to goal-setting and the adoption of new, effective strategies for personal betterment. Additionally, coach-ability strengthens relationships and communication, as it cultivates an environment of trust and mutual respect. By prioritizing coach-ability, we unlock our potential, meet our goals, and enjoy enriched personal and professional lives.

Part 3:

Coaching Others

CHAPTER 10
Coaching and Mentorship for Developing Coach-Ability

Do all the good you can, to all the people you can, as long as you can. — Anonymous[63]

COACHING AND MENTORSHIP ARE critical for developing coach-ability. In this chapter, we will discuss effective coaching and mentorship practices for developing coach-ability. We will explore how to create a supportive and safe environment for feedback and growth and how to develop strong relationships with coaches and mentors.

> **Challenge/Problem statement:** Even the most experienced leaders can struggle to develop coach-ability without effective coaching and mentorship practices that address their unique needs and learning styles.

1. Effective Coaching and Mentorship Practices

Effective coaching and mentorship practices are essential for developing coach-ability. These practices involve establishing clear goals, providing constructive feedback, and offering support and guidance. Effective coaches and mentors also help individuals develop self-awareness, challenge limiting beliefs, and develop new skills and strategies for growth.

High-Impact Leadership Begins with *You*! Our Actions Follow Our Values

The beginning of each New Year always allows me to reflect on the past year and plan for the upcoming year. My wife and I took a very relaxing vacation to Florida. On the plane ride there, I read *Judgment: How Winning Leaders Make Great Calls* by Noel M. Tichy and Warren G. Bennis.[64]

This book promised to be very interesting and full of gold nuggets concerning character education and how our character values affect the judgment calls we all have to make as leaders on a daily basis. I have always believed that leading with character first is the most important step any person can possibly take to live a healthy lifestyle worthy of example to others. I have even spoken about this subject called judgment during the seminars that focused on my climb up Mt. Ararat (altitude of 17,000 ft) in the late '80s.

Well, as fate would have it (and I believe there is a reason for everything that happens to us), on the last night of our vacation, my wife and I were enjoying a leisurely dinner before the New Year midnight festivities when my wife overheard a couple at another dinner table talking about a Florida University team that had recently expelled literally at least two dozen football players from the team because of cheating on an exam.[65]

At Deutsch's Gymnastics Training Center, we are passionate about helping to mold our athletes' characters by shaping their values and discipline, so you can imagine that this story was of real interest to me and a real shocker too. I could imagine one or two or even several players expelled for cheating—but dozens? I had never heard of such numbers before. However, I learned that at least half of this team of 60 or so players cheated on their online exam. That is both astounding and shocking!

What does that say about the leaders of the coaching staff as well as the leaders of the players themselves? Furthermore, it reminded me of one of my team captains at Deutsch's telling me that cheating was extremely prevalent at our local high school.

She also said that the teacher could do nothing to hold the kids accountable. So this kind of thing is not just happening in Florida. In this book on judgment, the authors made a case for the fact that *our actions always follow our values, and our values shape our character.*

I believe this kind of behavior is a very real problem in our society today and permeates its moral fabric. Somehow, we must have drifted so far off course as a culture and as a society that we no longer even recognize our own moral compass. How disappointing!

Do we not have the dignity and fortitude as a society, culture, and nation to recapture that moral compass? I want to encourage you to be courageous enough and determined to lead by example with character first. Each of us can make a difference in the lives and quality of lives of those around us.

To illustrate, even though we are just one individual (or seed), we can mentor and grow so many apples that we are not even aware of how many other people we affect and influence with our example of living life by leading with character first. I am reminded of what Robert Schuller once said: "Any fool can count the seeds in an apple. Only God can count all the apples in one seed."[66]

Let's make sure that each of us do everything we can to help all the apples we grow to develop great character. Lead with character first!

2. Creating a Supportive and Safe Environment for Feedback and Growth

Creating a supportive and safe environment for feedback and growth is critical for developing coach-ability. This involves establishing trust, being nonjudgmental (judgments to condemn), and creating a culture of open communication. Individuals should feel safe to ask questions, share their thoughts and feelings, and receive constructive feedback without fear of negative consequences.

A Story About the Dual Sides of Coach-Ability in IT Security

Being coach-able isn't just crucial for personal growth—it's essential for ensuring the safety and smooth running of our businesses too. In the tech world, especially in IT, security is paramount. I once had a client—we'll call him Jack—whose company we were tasked with cybersecurity protecting. We were responsible for securing their networks and facilitating smooth communication across their IT equipment and networks.

The company changed hands and the new CEO, Jack, not knowing me or my company very well, had his own thoughts about IT security. Despite my 30-plus years in the industry and countless tales of the importance of safeguarding networks, he dismissed my warnings as unnecessary, even referring to them as security sh*t.

The CEO believed he and his team were impervious to the threats I outlined because they felt they had nothing hackers valued worth stealing. This mindset, surprisingly common, often stems from a lack of understanding about what hackers truly want.

Moreover, I had always advocated for recognizing the human factor—our very own people—as the greatest potential threat to security. Hackers are very patient. It is like the old saying "We have the watches, but they have the time." Furthermore, hackers don't always want your data—they may be in your network to discover and find the money trail.

Reflecting on the Houdini concept (named after Harry Houdini, a great magician and escape artist), which purports that no lock is unbreakable, I hold firm that no network is 100% secure. Sometimes, the cracks appear where we least expect them—like in the actions of our own team. Clicking on a deceptive link or unknowingly violating password policies can open doors we strive to keep locked.

All it takes is for the bad guys to find one hole or weakness. We have to close all the holes, but the bad guys only need to find one.

So it just takes one person, the human factor, as the weakest link to not do something they should have done or do something they should not have done.

Bad guys are not interested in breaking through your defenses, such as firewalls, antivirus protection, or antimalware. They are interested in finding the weakest link, the human factor.

Jack, an apparently uncoach-able CEO, found himself in a tight spot two weeks later after disregarding my advice. He received an email claiming his laptop camera had been hacked and used to record his actions in his office over the last few weeks. The hacker demanded $5,000, threatening to release potentially damaging recordings to the internet if the money demanded wasn't paid. Jack was now being extorted.

I couldn't help but ponder two things. First, what was his view on "security sh*t" now? Second, what confidential activities or conversations might have been captured if his camera had been used to record office activities and conversations, considering he didn't follow our basic security protocol, including covering the camera when not in use?

Despite this, Jack's company continued to grow exponentially. Even after this alarming incident, he remains unswayed in his stance toward the necessity of IT security. His ongoing success seemingly affirms his belief that his company is immune to major security threats. Once the emergency is taken care of, uncoach-able leaders seem to always migrate back to their own arrogance and egotistical leadership methods.

If these types of people were good examples for their groups and companies to follow, they would exhibit one character skill in particular that allows leaders to always lead with character first.

That character skill is humility. Being humble allows the team to identify with them as someone just like them and to be a better listener, learner, and servant leader.

But here's the reality—stay uncoach-able, and you might get away with it for a while, but it only takes one breach to dismantle what took you years to build. In this CEO's case, six years later, a very shocking and painful event occurred after he quit using our company to provide security solutions for his company. His company was hit with ransomware. I was told they lost all their data, and they were out of business for months. Imagine that! A multi-million dollar per month company brought to their knees in a heartbeat. So, the moral of the story is to always be humble and hungry to learn, knowing that we are human becomings and we are the weakest link. We need others to be better than we can be by ourselves.

My friend, stay coach-able! It doesn't matter if you think the information isn't necessary at the moment. Being coach-able allows you to absorb information, keep it on file, and have it ready for when the time comes that you do need it. There's a quote attributed to the Roman philosopher Seneca that says, "Luck is when preparation meets opportunity." Ensuring your defenses are in order gives you the opportunity to prevent potential crises before they unfold. Some may think that luck is random, but maybe preparation makes us more lucky after all.

Trike on, and remember, leading with character first and keeping an open, coach-able mindset is often the key to ongoing learning, prevention, and timely solutions to security and privacy in this age of technologies driven by virtual reality and AI.

3. Developing Strong Relationships with Coaches and Mentors

Developing strong relationships with coaches and mentors is essential for coaching others effectively. This involves establishing rapport, building trust, and being committed to the coaching or mentoring relationship. Effective coaches and mentors should be reliable, accessible, and empathetic, and able to provide constructive feedback and support when needed.

Sometimes, finding a coach happens by accident, and sometimes it is planned. I want to share a story about a United States Air Force officer in Turkey (not the highest-ranking officer but an officer who had the highest position of power), who offered to coach and mentor me. On one occasion, I was at a chapel meeting for Bible study, and of course, this was after hours and off duty from our military jobs, so many of the people that came for the Bible study were simply in civilian clothes. That means if I did not know them or had never met them, I also would not know their rank, position, or job.

On this occasion, during the Bible study and prayer meeting, I shared that I had been offered a job to be the IT chief of maintenance (COM) for all the U.S. operations in Turkey. That means I would have about 1,200 people under my purview, and I would be responsible for billions of dollars of equipment and a budget worth millions of dollars. As if that wasn't stressful enough, the job offer was for a position that only two years earlier was a lieutenant colonel slot. Well, I was only a two-year captain.

I was very anxious and nervous because I had no idea how, as a two-year captain, I was going to fill the COM job without many more years of experience and without a higher rank. How would my people look to me for leadership? What would they think? Would they respect me and follow my lead? So many questions and seemingly no answers.

So once our Bible study was over, and we finished praying together, a person in civilian clothes came up to me and offered to mentor me. I had never met this person before, and as I already shared, I had no idea who he was, what rank he was, or what position he filled in his leadership role in Turkey. I accepted his offer, and we agreed that I would come to his office later that next week.

When I arrived at his office the next week, I found out that it was located in quite a large Turkish building. So I went in the front door and was immediately met by guards with machine guns and escorted to a little room where I was asked what I was there for and asked to sign in on a register. Once I told the officer in charge who I was scheduled to meet with, he immediately said something in Turkish, and you would have thought someone pulled the fire alarm. Every guard and every person within earshot of that officer's commands went into action and got very busy preparing for something, of which I had no idea.

I did not wait very long, and all of a sudden, everyone snapped to attention, and the whole area was quiet. All the hustle and bustle had stopped. I looked up the huge, ornately decorated staircase that was about 10 feet in width and covered in bright-red carpet, and an officer was coming down the stairs. As he neared the bottom of the stairs, I could see that it was the man I had met the week before at the Bible study and prayer meeting.

He was the person I was meeting with? He was the person who everyone had snapped to attention for? It was him. Oh my gosh! Now I did not know what to think. I could see that he had the rank of a full-bird colonel.

The colonel came over to greet me and asked me to follow him. He turned around, and much to my surprise, we were now both walking up the pristine staircase with the same red carpet I had just seen him walk down, but now it was under my feet. This was like in the movies. Who was this person, and what kind of power or position did he have? I had no idea, but I knew he was pretty high up, and by the way the guards and others reacted, he wielded some major power as well.

When we reached the top of the stairs, we turned left to walk down this amazing hallway with wonderful pictures and beautiful woodwork on both sides. We passed the first office, and then the colonel opened the second door to what turned out to be his office.

It was the biggest office I had ever seen. By now, I was mesmerized and feeling so small. I had no idea what I had gotten myself into. Once inside the door, the colonel closed it behind us, asked me to take a seat on the couch, and told me he would be right back.

He proceeded to walk over to his desk, which was the biggest desk I had ever seen. Now, I may be exaggerating, but from what I recall, his desk was made out of very pristine wood with ornate designs, and to the best of my recollection, it must have measured 10 feet in width and six feet in depth. There was hardly anything on the desk except a phone and a blotter. But on the corner of the desk, I could see what looked like a Bible, and the colonel grabbed the Bible and came back to the couch and took a seat on the other end across from me.

He proceeded to ask me questions about my job offer and what it would entail. Then he opened up the Bible and read to me a couple of passages from the Old Testament. After that, he started to ask me if I wanted the job and what I might be worried about in taking that position. We spent about an hour in his office, and all the while, he was not telling me anything about what I should do but asked really good questions and discussed with me what real leadership was all about. It was one of the most memorable mentoring experiences I have ever had. He was really coaching me.

Of course, I had asked for prayer but had no idea that anyone would volunteer to mentor and prepare me to make the most monumental decision of my life while also assisting me with a deeper understanding of what leadership was really all about.

When we were done, he escorted me back down to the front door of the building, and of course, all the guards snapped to attention when he approached them. He thanked me, wished me well, and let me know he was there for me. If I needed any more assistance, I could call on him at any time.

So, based on the session I had with him, I took the job. Now, I know it may seem strange, but I truly believe he was my guardian angel. Even today, I believe that since he had the top power position under one of the very top Turkish generals in the country, he may very well have put out the word that anyone on any of my bases, either on the U.S. or Turkish side, should do their best to help me help them be successful in our mission.

Most importantly, I knew his humility and leadership were genuine and authentic. Meeting with him was like it was meant to be, and he was my guardian angel. He was very encouraging and assured me that rank is not what people respect the most. It is the *leader who cares* who garners the most respect from their people.

I spent the next two years successfully working with my team from Iraq to Istanbul and from the Black Sea to the Mediterranean, running a very effective and efficient communications mission. Without his mentoring and guidance, I may never have taken that job. That would have meant that I would never have had the privilege of serving my people and making a difference for them, plus adding value and staying humble in their service. I would have thought I did not have the experience, rank, or skills. He made me feel I could do it, and I did. Actually, we, my team and I, did!

That is what a great leader does. There are great leaders (influencers) who also mentor or coach others. They pour into others like this colonel did for me. He helped me make the right career decision, and because of him, my team and I were successful, and we were also significant for others whom we served.

So, coaching and mentorship are critical for developing coach-ability. Effective coaching and mentorship practices, creating a supportive and safe environment for feedback and growth, and developing strong relationships with coaches and mentors can all help individuals develop the skills and attitudes needed to become more coach-able. Each individual can achieve their goals and unlock their full potential by working with effective coaches and mentors.

I want to wrap up this chapter by sharing with you that if I had not been humble in my position, as this colonel was, I may never have learned what I needed to lead and manage the largest COM job in the world. You see, my people were my best teachers and coaches—and I learned that they loved to coach their leaders to be smart and be better than they could be without them on their team. What an amazing learning experience. As my dad always said, "Your people are your backbone. Don't you ever forget that." And I didn't. Thank you, Dad, thank you, Colonel, and thank you, team.

Keep trikin', team!

Chalk Talk Coaching Tip

Effective coaching and mentorship are pivotal in cultivating coach-ability, which is about more than skill development—it's a foundation for ethical leadership and personal integrity. By setting clear goals, embracing feedback, and challenging limiting beliefs, individuals can grow their self-awareness and strategies for success, aligning actions with core values, such as humility, to lead by example both professionally and personally.

- **Promise of solution:** Committing to a structured coaching and mentorship program promises to enhance leader coach-ability through personalized goal-setting, feedback, and the development of a growth mindset.

- **Suggested action step**: Identify a coach or mentor who exemplifies the leadership qualities you aspire to develop. Initiate a mentoring relationship with scheduled monthly sessions to review progress, set specific goals, and receive tailored feedback and guidance.

Note: Remember to fill in the blanks and reflect deeply on the questions provided to get the most out of these workbook questions at the end of each chapter. Coach-ability isn't just about learning new strategies—it's also about introspection, self-reflection, and understanding how interactions with our coaches and mentors can shape us and grow our character skills.

Workbook for Coach-Ability, Chapter 10

Coaching and Mentorship for Developing Coach-Ability

Fill-in-the-Blanks

1. Effective coaching and mentorship practices are essential for developing _____. These practices involve establishing clear goals, providing constructive feedback, and offering support and guidance.

2. A strong relationship with a coach or mentor can provide a _____ and safe environment, encouraging open communication and growth.

3. One essential character skill and a quality of effective coaches and mentors is _____, which can help individuals navigate through personal and professional growth.

Reflective Questions

1. Think about a time when a coach or mentor provided you with guidance. How did their feedback help you grow, and what specific steps did you take as a result?

2. Reflect on an experience where you resisted the advice of a mentor or coach. In hindsight, how might a coach-able attitude have changed the outcome or process?

3. Consider the role that trust plays in a coaching or mentorship relationship. Can you identify a situation where trust (or lack thereof) affected your ability to receive and act upon guidance?

Summary of Chapter 10 Workbook

In chapter 10, we learn about the transformative power of coaching and mentorship in developing coach-ability. Effective coaching practices that include setting clear objectives, offering constructive critique, and maintaining supportive guidance are key to fostering growth. Strong relationships with coaches and mentors, rooted in trust and commitment, lay the groundwork for significant personal and professional advancement. Through the lessons and insights gained in this chapter, individuals are encouraged to remain open and receptive to guidance and to grow their character skills such as humility, thereby enabling them to navigate life's challenges with greater resilience and adaptability.

CHAPTER 11
How to Encourage Coach-Ability in Others

Whether you believe you can do a thing or not, you are right.— Henry Ford[67]

ENCOURAGING COACH-ABILITY IN OTHERS is essential for creating a positive and supportive work environment. In this chapter, we will explore how to encourage coach-ability in others, including creating a positive and encouraging environment, celebrating progress and small wins, and encouraging learning goals and feedback by seeking and practicing effective communication and active listening.

> **Challenge/Problem statement:** When we encourage coach-ability in others, we often face the hurdle of creating an environment where individuals feel safe and supported in pursuing personal growth and development.

1. Creating a Positive and Encouraging Environment

Creating a positive and encouraging environment is essential for encouraging coach-ability in others. This involves being kind, positive, optimistic, and supportive of others. Leaders should provide opportunities for growth and development, offer constructive feedback, and recognize the efforts of team members.

Navigating Integrity

Rules and regulations are established for a reason. Many times, they are there as a framework to guide us safely and creatively to our goals, desires, and dreams. Regardless of the outcome of the circumstance, if we are kind and really want the best for others, we can influence them far greater than we ever thought possible. A fascinating illustration of this emerged after I graduated from officer training school in Biloxi, Mississippi, specializing in communication electronics.

Subsequently, I was selected to join the Tactical Air Warfare Center with the 727 Tech Control Squadron (TCS) at Eglin Air Force Base on Hurlburt Field. While stationed there, I not only learned about implementing communication electronics in practice but also absorbed valuable lessons about leadership through observing various officers and NCOs. Particularly, I really started to grasp the importance of leading with character. Leadership isn't merely about technical training or managing communication, electronics, management, or teamwork. It encompasses character-driven leadership as well.

A vivid memory from my time at the 727th TCS involves an incident with the Company Grade Officer Council (CGOC)—the advisor to the CGOC organization that I belonged to, which included all the captains and lieutenants from that base. During one of our monthly meetings, I decided to run for president. I'd been encouraged to run and felt optimistic about my chances.

However, I was informed that several officers, who had never attended the meetings, intended to show up on election day to vote, and maybe one of them might even run against me for president. This struck me as odd since our regulations clearly stated that attendance at a certain number of consecutive meetings was mandatory to vote or run for a position. Undeterred, because the regulations and policies would not allow someone who had not attended to run for office, I shrugged off the warning and proceeded to participate in the election.

On election day, I presented my campaign, but so did some unfamiliar faces, including an officer who was also running for president, but who I knew hadn't attended the prerequisite number of meetings that qualified him to run for office. I questioned the advisor on this, referencing our policies, but the advisor, a veteran lieutenant colonel with years of experience, disregarded my objections and proceeded with the vote.

Predictably, I lost to the officer who hadn't previously attended. I lost primarily because he had brought a good number of his friends (who were also officers and had not attended meetings either) to vote for him. Again, this was against the organization's charter of rules and policies. This not only defied our regulations but showcased a lack of character on the advisor's part. He knew the rules but allowed the election to proceed unfairly and improperly.

So what does this teach us? First, the advisor placed greater importance on having a pilot (which I was not) as president of the council rather than adhering to principles. Second, even if he felt some guilt—which I'll illustrate he might have had—he chose to act against his conscience, possibly due to external pressures.

A couple of months later, I entered a triathlon. I trained really hard for this race, even adding extra weight to my bicycle by securing my young son's baby seat to it. On race day, I noticed the CGOC advisor observing me from the shoreline as we prepared to swim in the Gulf off Eglin Air Force Base. Our eyes met several times, and I perceived a sense of guilt in his glances, likely recalling the unjust election he facilitated. Fun fact—I placed third in that triathlon, and it was the first triathlon I had ever participated in.

As I reflect on the broader context (including the base personnel during their preparation and deployment to the Grenada military conflict), it's imperative to have leaders who act with character, especially in times of conflict. Adhering to regulations, be they international laws or localized policies, and allowing our conscience to guide our actions are paramount.

In conclusion, while rules and regulations provide a structured framework, they are only as good as our character and conscience. Our character and conscience are our true navigators. This concept encapsulates the Tricycle Effect—leading with character first and ensuring that our moral compass guides our journey in all aspects of life.

2. Celebrating Progress and Small Wins

Celebrating progress and small wins is essential for encouraging coach-ability in others. By recognizing the efforts and achievements of team members, individuals are more likely to feel motivated and engaged. Celebrating progress and small wins can also help build confidence and a sense of accomplishment.

In our gym and at our IT company, we always had bells to celebrate small and big wins and victories. At the gym, we have a normal-looking brass bell we purchased in Turkey, knowing that someday after we returned from military life, we would start a gymnastics club and help athletes celebrate their wins.

At our IT company (located in Wisconsin), we used a very large cowbell. Even after I sold the IT company, I kept that cowbell and have it at home.

Over the years, using the bells at our IT company and at the gym has been very motivational for our people, athletes, and teams. It seems like a simple concept, but even small, simple pats on the back to reward performance make a monumental difference in esprit de corps and morale. It is amazing to learn how hard people will work as individuals and as teams to have the joy and opportunity to ring the bell so they can boast about their wins and accomplishments with their teammates.

Both bells accomplished the same purpose: to reward and celebrate wins.

Small wins aggregately add up sometimes to more than most big wins. My 8- to 12-year-olds love to ring the bell in the gym, especially if it is the first time they have made a skill. If they make a skill for the very first time, we have them ring the bell and then come right back and demonstrate to everyone that it wasn't a fluke. They really did get it. And they love it when everyone stops what they are doing to watch them and cheer them on to success. As coaches, we love to stop everyone and have them focus on that one little athlete in the gym so that athlete knows that the coaches and teammates care about their success and, more importantly, care about them as teammates!

After all the failures over the time that it takes to learn a skill, once the skill is learned successfully, those athletes do deserve a celebration.

So why don't we consistently celebrate small wins and victories? I think it's a cultural mindset. We grow up and think it is below us to do such a thing. Celebrating little things is for kids, and after all, we are adults now that we are in the workforce.

It pays to change that mindset.

In the business world, too often we get or earn a win, and we simply graze over it and then quickly move on to the next thing. We need to stop, take a breath, and savor the success for a moment for the individual and the team.

I saw the same thing in adults (big kids) who would ring the bell after a sale at our IT company that sometimes took weeks or months to win, with a technology challenge that employees finally solved, or after any number of successful efforts. Just like the kids in our gym, the big kids would smile ear to ear as well, and they enjoyed the moment too!

Don't count the small wins out either. Each small win, just as each small step climbing up Mt. Ararat got us to the peak, is worth celebrating, and so are your wins that take successful small steps toward your goals in life and business.

There are lots of ways to celebrate too. You can give high fives, shake hands, hug someone, praise them in front of their peers, take time to have drinks or snacks and reminisce, create certificates, give company or team gifts, celebrate birthdays or special accomplishments with a cookout, give an extra day off without notice, and many, many more. Be creative and learn what motivates you, your people, and your teams. Once you learn what motivates your team, you will find they will get behind you and support you in ways you never dreamed of. That is why people build dream teams.

Ring the bell, my friend, and trike on!

3. Encouraging Learning Goals and Feedback Seeking

Encouraging learning goals and feedback seeking is essential for encouraging coach-ability in others. Leaders should encourage team members to set learning goals, seek feedback, and be open to constructive criticism. By creating a culture of learning and growth, individuals are more likely to develop their skills and unlock their full potential.

The Impact of Unseen Influence and Steadfast Grit

Imagine this: Leadership isn't always about the conscious efforts we make to guide others. Sometimes, it sneaks into the unexpected moments of our interactions, silently shaping the paths of those we touch.

> As John C. Maxwell beautifully encapsulates, "Leadership is influence, nothing more, nothing less."[2]

I want to share a story about feedback, influence, commitment, and unwavering grit from the early days of our gymnastics training center back in Wisconsin.

Before my wife and I opened the doors to our gym on June 1, 1990, we knew our mission wasn't just to mold young gymnasts but to weave a thread of character, leadership, and moral values into their upbringing—all without explicitly saying so verbally. In our gym, banners proudly display character skill values and virtues like trustworthiness, respect, responsibility, fairness, caring, and citizenship, quietly whispering the deeper purpose we are fervently passionate about.

We landed in a small town with fewer than 9,000 residents, where my parents lived and had grown up, and our journey in business began. Not long after opening, I was invited to speak at a local men's club meeting. The invitation was a great opportunity to share our passion and the essence of our new business venture. However, a stark comment from one of the town's leaders before the meeting even started threw a brief shadow over my glowing ember of enthusiasm.

He said, "You won't last six months."

Imagine hearing that feedback when you're bubbling with excitement and purpose. As if just starting out in business wasn't nerve-racking enough.

But if there's one thing that wasn't in short supply, it was our grit. Our commitment. My wife and I didn't just survive for the first six months—we have now thrived in our little gym business for 34 years, touching the lives of thousands of children and families, imparting not just gymnastics skills but also lessons in leadership, communication, and most importantly, character skills.

According to the Bureau of Labor Statistics, about 45% of businesses never make it beyond five years. They also say that only 25% of businesses make it to 15 years or more.[69] It takes more than technical capability to make it over the long haul in any business. There are so many variables and unknowns that come at business owners. People skills like teamwork, communication, and leadership are so very important as well. But the most important business skills are the character skills like grit, courage, and persistence! Negative feedback can come in all varieties, shapes, and sizes. Many times, the deck of cards is stacked against us. We still need to stay positive and look for the good in every situation. That is easier said than done, I know, but true. However, it is also true that even negative feedback can be taken constructively if interpreted and used appropriately.

Talk about character skills, grit, courage, and persistence—Jesus Christ was the ultimate example of a leader and, even more so, a highly effective servant leader.

As I was writing this chapter, my daughter-in-law, Ashley Deutsch, introduced me to the book *Jesus, CEO*. Ashley was given this book as required reading as part of her education and training as a nurse practitioner in school at Concordia University in Wisconsin. In her book, J*esus, CEO*, author Laurie Beth Jones uses Jesus Christ as the ultimate leader by example and showcases the Omega leadership style, which she says, "transcends the best of the Alpha (masculine) and Beta (feminine) leadership styles."[70]

In our gym, character, grit, and competence became the trilogy of our teaching. While talent occasionally walked through our doors, it was those with a hunger, a burning commitment, and a relentless pursuit of their goals, who stuck around and soared to the highest levels of gymnastics.

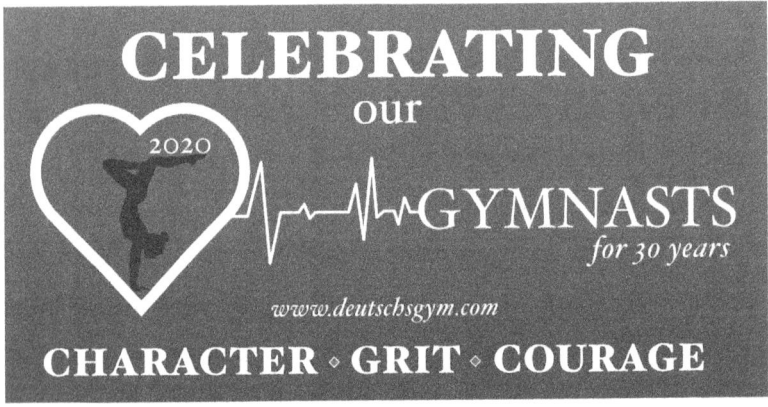

When I ask any of my athletes as they are beginning their gymnastics careers, "Are you hungry?" I'm seeking to uncover a depth of determination and commitment beneath the surface. It's not just about talent or skill—it's more about the desire and the fire that blazes within.

Are you hungry, my friend? What fire lies inside you that motivates you to be so passionate that nothing will stop you from getting to your goal? If you are not able to answer that question, then maybe it is time to step back and reflect on what really counts in life. And, when I say reflect, don't just reflect with your head—reflect with your heart. What gives you meaning and purpose in life? What energizes you and excites you about life? That is most likely where you should be. We are here on this earth for a very short period of time, and what we do with that time can make a difference if we focus on adding value to others. Too often, I hear people say they are just trying to make it through the day or that they are just coasting in life. That is so very sad to hear. God did not make you to coast through life. He made you to be a champion in life. So, if you are leading in life with your heart and practicing your character skills, you will be able to overcome any obstacle that comes your way, because you will just see it as a stepping-stone in your journey called life.

Looking back, I can see how the ripple of our influence extended quietly but profoundly through our community. Today, in our gym, we have moms (previous gym daughters) who now bring their daughters to our gym, because they want their children to have the same experience they had. Recently, I reconnected with a dad (also a doctor) who came to our gym with his daughter decades earlier. He shared a story about his daughter, who also was on our very first team in 1991. This dad shared with me that he was at a recent gymnastics meet in Minnesota with his 45-year-old daughter and his granddaughter. His granddaughter was a level-six gymnast and was on a team that was also hours away from our gym. I had lost touch with this dad since his daughter had left our gym decades ago. So, in his story, this dad, with tears rolling down his cheeks, let me know how wonderful it was when he and his daughter realized that Kathy, my wife and also a gymnastics judge, was judging the meet.

He said to me, "I was overwhelmed to see my forty-five-year-old daughter quickly descend the bleachers at the end of the meet and run after Kathy like a little girl again to catch her coach and say hello." After all these years, he and his daughter still have fond memories of being on our team at Deutsch's Gym. Of course, once one of our gym daughters has been in our gym, they are always our gym daughter, and we like to say that it is still their home away from home. We still consider them a part of the Deutsch family.

So, we helped shape the lives of our little athletes and their futures, as well as others outside our gym, now that our athletes are grown-up, healthy citizens contributing to our communities. Just think, if we'd let the city leader's feedback and prediction dampen our spirit, thousands of children and families would have missed experiencing gymnastics and the depth of character we've taught, coached, and shared with them over many decades.

My friends, understand this: Your influence permeates through every interaction, silently leading and guiding others. Your life is so very important to others, unseen sometimes, but immeasurably influential. So, no matter what kind of feedback you receive, no matter who crosses your path, follow your heartstrings and be conscious of the silent waves of influence you can create to help others be successful and, more importantly, significant in life.

In previous chapters, we discussed body language and self-talk as part of feedback. To build on that, I also shared how visualization helps to create reality through feedback with the law of attraction. Those are tools and techniques you can practice to help you effectively journey through life by leading with your heart and character skills to attract other people and the riches in life that you deserve.

Let's build on this concept even further. Your body language and touch are so very important to others but also to yourself and in coaching yourself. The simple act of smiling at someone generally attracts a return smile. When we smile, we elicit chemicals in our brains that move us to think and act in accordance with the feeling we get from the effect of those chemicals. When those people we smile at smile back, we are helping them elicit chemicals in their brains and potentially changing how they feel as well. More importantly, there are people who hunger for someone to simply notice they are alive, and we can notice others just with our smile to them.

To bring this concept of smile to life, here is a story from the *New Yorker* about jumpers,[71] and even one story from the *New Yorker* that was recapped by Kripa Jayakumar, and it reads like this:

A man in his 30s once jumped off from the Golden Gate bridge. When investigations were done, it was found in his bureau, back at his home, a piece of note that read:

"I'm going to walk to the bridge. If at least one person smiles at me on the way, I will not jump."

That is one article I still remember to this day, which had the power to move me. We could have really prevented that suicide. We really could have helped him.

A smile was all it would have taken to save his life."

I want to encourage you through this story, that the impact and influence you can have on others does not happen only when you are physically present with someone. This powerful truth happens even when you and I are talking to someone over a phone, when we can't see them, or virtually online when we can see them but are still not physically present in the same room as them.

Here is a funny thing I like to do for people who answer the phone call I make with them. I only do this authentically and genuinely, so it is not on each phone call, but when I do this, I really mean it. Sometimes when I call someone, or even when they call me, I can immediately tell just through the intonation of their voice if they are having a good day, if they like what they are doing, and if they are excited about talking with me. However, most of the time, people are so busy and caught up in doing things, they forget to humanize their actions and events. So, if warranted, I sometimes tell the person at the other end of the phone line, "I can hear you smiling." That statement, all by itself, generally gets a response, and you can literally hear the other person perk up and respond with an even cheerier voice. This mirroring event is very powerful and adds value to the other person in a way that nothing else can.

Adding to the smile, we can influence others through our words as well. I come to the gym every day at 6:00 p.m. I only coach the team kids, and their practices begin late in the day. Therefore, the majority of the day is over, and yet we still have three hours of practice to go through. As I enter the gym, I am cognizant of the fact that I need to set the tone for that night's practice, no matter what has happened in each athlete's life earlier in the day. To do that, I always come in the door and say, "Good morning, team." Many times, I will even acknowledge individual athletes by name: "Good morning, Sarah!" Well, you can imagine, when the kids first start out at our gym, and they hear this message, they want to tell me that it is not morning. "Okay," I tell them, "but it is morning somewhere in the world, and at this moment, it is like morning for me to see you for the first time today."

After they understand why I say good morning, from then on, they normally respond, "Good morning, Dane!" Just helping them to know that every moment in life counts and they matter to me. Very refreshing!

Our voices are important, and so is physical touch. I haven't mentioned touch much yet in this book, but coaching ourselves and others can be most effective when we move beyond our words and provide a physical touch with others, such as shaking hands, tapping someone on the top of their head or shoulder, or a giving a good, solid hug. A physical touch from the heart also makes people feel better about themselves and, as a result, feel better about others and life in general. I believe we are made of energy, and when we touch others, we can effectively add to their energy. After all, I shared with you that we are human becomings. We are also spiritual becomings. We are all on the same journey in life, both physically and spiritually. If we go back to the *Jesus, CEO* book and use Jesus Christ as an example, one of the major things he did in His ministry was based on touch. He communicated *care* with touch, He healed with *love* by touch, He influenced others with His *trust* by touch, He raised the dead with His powerful *empathy* by touch and much more. Notice something? Every physical touch was the expression of His Christ character: care, love, trust, empathy, etc. Christ led others by example through the power of His character, and so can we. This truth will change your life, my friend! You, too, can live life growing and becoming a champion of character!

Stay resilient, commit to your dreams and passions, and in every step and even a stumble, remember to stay coach-able and trike on!

4. Practicing Effective Communication and Active Listening

Practicing effective communication and active listening is essential for encouraging coach-ability in others. Leaders need to listen actively, provide constructive feedback, and be open to hearing different perspectives. Effective communication and active listening can help build trust, establish rapport, and create a culture of trust, openness, and collaboration.

Here is a short story to help you learn to stop "don't-ing" yourself and be a champion of character.

The balance beam offers only a narrow four inches to perform on, whether it's walking, tumbling, dancing, or leaping. Often, coaches might advise, "Don't fall," or discourage other undesirable outcomes.

Here's the catch: As I pointed out earlier, this approach keeps the focus on the negative, not steering it toward what needs to happen to succeed.

Instead of *Don't do this* or *Don't do that*, imagine the difference when the guidance is *Keep your legs tight*, or *Finish strong*, or *Good focus now*.

When we emphasize what not to do, it disrupts the gymnast's learning to craft a positive self-dialogue or self-talk when communicating with themselves. So instead of advising *Don't fall*, what if we emphasize *Focus on the beam's end*? Or we could encourage the gymnast to remind themselves to stay tight. Guiding yourself toward desired outcomes—like not falling or avoiding wobbles and skillfully completing routines—makes a world of difference.

Ponder this: In my gymnastics coaching experience, when an athlete dwells on not doing something, their mind naturally gravitates toward the very thing they want to avoid. The same thing happens to us generally in life. Here, again, is where self-talk comes to the rescue. We need to be mindful of our self-talk and evaluate it for its positivity or negativity. If it is negative, we need to stop it and reframe the talk so it is positive. To really bring that concept home, let me share with you a story of a friend of mine who was a pharmacist—and a very good one too! At one point, he shared with me his negative self-talk that sometimes happens when he is filling a prescription.

Evidently, he sometimes worried he would get the wrong prescription filled for someone or count a number incorrectly. This was very disconcerting for him. He shared that he never ever had negative things that actually happened, but the needless worry was getting to him. So, I suggested he use a technique to jolt his negative thinking back to reality. I told him that he could make that jolt happen himself by wearing a rubber band on his wrist. Then I told him that each time he was speaking to himself negatively with his self-talk, as soon as he caught his negative thoughts, he should reach across to the wrist with the rubber band, pull it away from the wrist, and then let it go so it would snap his wrist. Once the jolt was applied, then he needed to reframe the message in his mind. Guess what? He tried it, and it worked perfectly. He felt so relieved since he had learned how he could harness that voice in his head to focus on productive thoughts. Now, I have no idea how many times a day he snaps his wrist, but I am willing to bet it has become less frequent over time.

This concept is so powerful that many books have been written about self-talk. One book I read recently is titled *Soundtracks*, and it is written by Jon Acuff.[72] In that book, he explains that we all have soundtracks running through our thoughts. So, it is very important that we exchange the broken soundtracks with good soundtracks or what I call soundtrack clips. In our gym, we now use soundtrack clips to refer to small, short phrases we tell ourselves, like *I can do this, I will get it eventually, one more step closer*, and so many more. My gymnasts and I actually study our self-talk and soundtracks. As I shared earlier in this book, the self-talk or soundtracks we dialogue inside ourselves actually foretell the outcome of our efforts. Good soundtracks and self-talk allow us to grow and perform up to our real potential. It takes effort, discipline, and grit to talk to yourself with good soundtracks and self-talk. Jon outlines three things that will help us identify good, healthy soundtrack clips.

1. Is what we are thinking truthful?

2. Is what we are saying to ourselves helpful?

3. Is what we are thinking about ourselves kind?[73]

Furthermore, Jon goes on to say, "There are three actions to change your thoughts from a super problem into a superpower."[74] The three *R*s can actually give us a process to establish tiny habits that help us monitor and manage our thoughts:

1. Retire (stop saying it).

2. Replace (use a healthy soundtrack clip).

3. Repeat (keep saying it to ourselves).[75]

Once we establish the tiny habits of the three *R*s, we can really rise up to the potential that we are capable of and make our thoughts a superpower, as Jon says. In our gym, now if an athlete hears another teammate sounding off with bad soundtracks and self-talk, we tell them to flip the clip. Fun huh? You can flip the clip in your head as well. Gymnasts are great at flipping!

> Your thoughts empower your actions, which in turn generate your results.— Jon Acuff[10]

Now, speaking of results, it just so happens that self-talk works equally well, and even more importantly, in business with our professional lives. Much like a *return on assets*, there is actually a *return on character*. Let me introduce you to return on character. Fred Kiel, co-founder of KRW International, wrote a book titled *Return on Character*. In the book, Fred asserts that character can actually be measured, and they are the first company in the world to actually do research quantitatively to "offer concrete reasons for rethinking our ideas about effective leadership, and to map out the direct connection between strong character, principled behavior, and sustainable business results."[77] It turns out that we can actually "describe the observable, consistent, and measurable relationship between character habits and organizational performance, risk, and engagement"[78] and demonstrate that the higher the character skills a leader has, the more successful the return on character is. There actually can be a big return on assets if we lead with character skills first! So, character is truly the foundation of leadership and now it can be demonstrated quantitatively through the research that KRW has done.

Furthermore, in the KRW training, they refer to Duhigg's habit loop.[79] "KRW Return on Character, What Is Character, Study Guide #1" says, "Habit loops include routines that are measurable." Just like *Soundtracks*, the study guide goes on to say, "Charles Duhigg tells us that habits are created in a specific pattern he calls the 'habit loop.'"[80]

The habit loop consists of three elements: the cue, the routine, and the reward.[81] The KRW study guide #1 goes on to say, "For years, people have focused on the routine, but what is really important is the cue and the reward. By identifying a cue and providing your brain with a strong enough reward, you can teach yourself any new habit."[82]

I hope it is becoming very clear that not only can we establish good soundtracks in our self-talk, but we can actually establish solid habit loops to create character skills that form the foundation of our leadership. We can absolutely measure it, and those tools can help us to reach our full potential and become champions of character.

We all battle with our self-talk consciously and unconsciously. The good news is we can control it, and we can win the battles with our self-talk and our habits. In our gym, I don't talk "techie" too often with my athletes, but I do want them to get the benefit of some of this coaching about self-talk, and I don't want them to see their thoughts as their enemy or a threat to them. So, we use the phrase *monkeys in the head*. They can easily wrap their minds around monkeys running around in their heads. It's kind of like the movie *Jumanji* when the monkeys took over the police cars in the town on one of the results of rolling the dice. Now, here's a real learning gem for you. Our brains have a tendency toward negativity bias.[83] Did you know that? You most likely did but had not thought consciously about that before. Therefore, reducing negative thinking may propel us further than just incorporating positive thinking, because negative thinking is actually about four to seven times more influential than positive self-talk![84] In other words, if we reduce the number of monkeys or negative thoughts in our head, we can improve our self-talk, and in turn, our behavioral outcomes will be more effective rather than simply using positive self-talk. If we establish habits on top of good soundtrack clips, then we get double the advantage. So, get control of the monkeys in your head.

Figure 1—Negative Thought Self-Sabotage—The Waltline Group

If we apply this principle to our own self-coaching toward not just success but also significance, wherein we bring value to others, it creates a transformative ripple. Since you and I are individuals of value who appreciate people and enhance their worth, it becomes imperative to mute those negative thoughts. Simultaneously, while maintaining a positive attitude is crucial, stifling negativity wields a mightier power than just sprinkling in isolated positive thoughts.

So the next time intrusive thoughts sneak in, snip the negativity in the bud. Avoid telling yourself, Don't think like that, because much like the beam scenario, if you think, Don't fall, your brain processes *fall*, and you fail. If you assert, Don't be afraid, your mind visualizes fear.

The golden ticket? Direct your self-talk toward the outcomes you seek to manifest: I will hold my balance on the beam. I will conclude with vigor. My leap will be stable." These affirmations radiate far more positivity than mere admonitions of *Don't do this* or *Don't do that*.

While staying positive is integral and fostering a cheerful attitude is vital, make a concerted effort to capture every thought, replace it with a productive thought, and diminish negativity. You'll radiate positivity more strongly than ever before.

With that, coach yourself like a champion of character and—trike on, team!

In conclusion, encouraging coach-ability in others requires creating a positive and encouraging environment, celebrating progress and small wins, encouraging learning goals and feedback seeking, and practicing effective communication and active listening. By encouraging coach-ability in others, leaders can build a more engaged, motivated, and high-performing team.

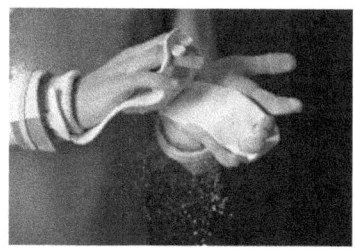

Chalk Talk Coaching Tip

In fostering coach-ability, it is crucial to establish a foundation of integrity and character-driven leadership that will resonate and inspire others, even amid challenges. Recognize and reward the small victories and consistent character-driven self-talk and habits with the efforts of your team, as this not only boosts morale but also solidifies a collective commitment to growth and excellence. Your culture of the organization will benefit as well!

- **Promise of solution:** By fostering an environment that celebrates every small victory and provides constructive feedback, we promise to cultivate a culture where coach-ability thrives, and team members are motivated to actively seek growth opportunities.

- **Suggested action step**: Implement a small-wins bell in your work environment where team members can literally ring in their achievements, no matter how small, fostering a sense of accomplishment and encouraging a continual feedback loop.

Workbook for Coach-Ability, Chapter 11

How to Encourage Coach-Ability in Others

Fill-in-the-Blanks

1. Creating a positive and encouraging environment is essential for coach-ability, which involves being kind, positive, _____, and supportive of others.

2. Leaders should provide opportunities for growth and _____, offer constructive feedback, and recognize team members' efforts.

3. In fostering coach-ability, recognizing and celebrating _____ and small wins are as important as acknowledging big victories.

Reflective Questions

1. Reflect on a time when someone encouraged your growth. How did their support and feedback affect your

development and willingness to learn?

2. Consider your reaction to small wins. How do you celebrate them, and how might increasing recognition of these moments enhance coach-ability in your environment?

3. Recall a situation where your influence, either direct or indirect, had a noticeable impact on someone else. How did this experience shape your understanding of the role character plays in leadership?

Summary of Chapter 11 Workbook

Chapter 11 underscores the importance of encouraging coach-ability in creating a robust and supportive work environment. It stresses the need for leaders to craft an atmosphere of positivity and optimism, offering opportunities for growth and development through constructive feedback and the recognition of team efforts. It is through such a nurturing environment that individuals are motivated to seek feedback, set learning goals, and engage in effective communication. Celebrating every achievement, no matter the size, builds a culture of accomplishment and continual learning. The chapter also highlights the profound influence of character-driven leadership through self-talk and habits, and the ripple effect it has within a community, reinforcing that leadership is as much about silent influence as it is about direct guidance.

CHAPTER 12
Coach-Ability in Leadership

Feedback is the breakfast of champions. — Ken Blanchard[85]

BEING COACH-ABLE IS AN essential skill for effective leadership. In this chapter, we will discuss how coach-ability can improve leadership skills, including how to use feedback effectively and how to empower and mentor team members.

> Challenge/Problem statement: The challenge is to enhance leadership skills by fostering a culture of coach-ability where leaders effectively use feedback to grow themselves and their team members, fostering an environment of continual improvement and mentoring.

1. Using Feedback Effectively

Using feedback effectively is critical for improving leadership skills. Coach-able leaders are more humble, open to feedback, and better equipped to use it to improve their performance. Effective leaders practice humility and use feedback to identify areas for improvement, set goals, develop new skills and strategies, and most importantly, coach others to be leaders.

It's important for leaders to coach other people to be leaders. Otherwise, without leader coaches, no one will purposefully and intentionally coach someone to carry on with whatever is important in both our personal and professional lives. That is our main goal in our gym. We have two formal apprenticeship programs in our gym: USA Gymnastics Judging and Gymnastics Coaching.

On top of those two programs, through the sport of gymnastics (both recreational and competitive sport), we focus on coaching youth and children to develop and grow up as productive and healthy adults to become moms, dads, lawyers, doctors, dentists, homeschooling parents, military veterans, as well as leaders in whatever career field they choose to follow. That is our big, hairy, audacious goal (BHAG).[86]

We are growing leaders for the future. More than that, we are growing and developing leaders with character now. We are building leaders who truly understand how to lead with character first in everything they do. We simply use gymnastics as the vehicle to teach them character skills, people skills, and technical skills, all the while learning how to acquire grit, lead with character first, and live by the Golden Rule.

So, the underlying point to effective feedback is that we stay coach-able by being humble and working hard to provide the necessary feedback for our athletes and students to grow and develop in all areas of the Tricycle Effect: character skills wheel, competence skills wheel (technical and people skills), and the seat of courage.

Just as we have body language that motivates us, sometimes feedback through the power of touch is extremely powerful. I have touched on this briefly in chapter 11. Touch is what I call the unspoken power of a personal high five.

It's interesting how a simple gesture can make a massive difference. Throughout my years coaching gymnastics, I've stumbled upon a fascinating observation. On nights when I consistently give the kids high fives, whether their attempts are successful or not, something remarkable happens—their ability to perform a skill improves markedly.

So what's going on here? I've come to believe that touch, even in its simplest form between humans, becomes its own motivational force. No words are required. When we physically connect with another person, there's this vibrant energy that silently communicates positivity and encouragement, and it's a revitalizing force that energizes us and boosts our ability to succeed in various pursuits—be it in sports, business, or our personal lives.

Let me share a bit of an experiment I conducted many years ago. On certain nights, I intentionally refrained from giving the kids or athletes high fives or providing encouraging pats on the back or top of the head during warm-ups.

What I found is that the vibe of the practice would take a noticeable dip in energy and, in turn, performance—and it was noticeable. Some nights, I discovered that when I would give the athletes high fives or touch their heads or shoulders, I could actually get the entire team into a flow state, and everyone's capability to work out at peak-performance levels improved.

The power of touch was an amazing discovery. It is not something new, but for me, it was a personal coaching experience and discovery that I could actually understand and own. I could coach others simply through the power of touch.

Typically, I greet every one of my athletes while they are warming up. I might pat them on the shoulder, tap them on the top of their heads, tease them slightly, and of course, dole out high fives.

For some, I kneel down right in front of them, look them right in the eyes, and tell them, "I am so happy you are here with us tonight!" For all I know, this might be the only personal attention they received all day. As I navigate through each of the kids warming up in the gym, I keep this in mind, ensuring each touch and interaction communicates two things: "You matter to me." "You are somebody with value!" Some days, I can hardly wait to see them, to high-five them, and to say with sincerity, "I'm glad you're here with me."

You see, embracing our humanity—our "humaneness," if you will—is crucial. So, here's a gentle reminder for you: Coaching others extends beyond verbal instruction. Sometimes, we can coach profoundly with just a meaningful touch, and no words are needed at all.

Over the years, some of my athletes might be way across the gym, but once we make eye contact, we know exactly what each other is thinking, like *good focus, be aggressive, go hard*, or any number of other communiqués we use to get the athlete in a state of flow for peak performance.

A human touch, brimming with genuine care and authenticity, can communicate what might take thousands of words to convey otherwise. You've likely heard the saying "A picture is worth a thousand words." I'd often add, "A video is worth ten thousand words." However, in my eyes, a heartfelt human touch transcends them all, potentially being worth hundreds of thousands of words.

Children, especially, can perceive whether you genuinely care, often through your touch and mere presence. They can feel your care and concern. They know if you care from the heart or if you are just putting on a show or going through the motions.

So, reach out to those around you with a heartfelt touch. Create connections by extending a hand, by looking others in the eye, and by letting them know that you really care and that they truly matter.

All right, team, let's head out there, build and grow those heartfelt connections, make a tangible difference, and as always, trike on!

2. Empowering Team Members

Empowering and mentoring team members is another critical aspect of leadership. Leaders who are humble, coach-able, and teachable are more likely to empower and mentor their team members, which can help to build trust and collaboration. Empowering team members involves providing them with the tools and resources they need to succeed and supporting them in their development. Mentoring team members involves providing guidance, support, and feedback to help them achieve their goals.

It is one thing to simply teach someone something, and it is an entirely different thing to equip someone with something.

> Teaching is generally one direction, teacher to student. Coaching is bidirectional—teacher to student and student to teacher.

Equipping is different again because besides equipping encompassing teaching and coaching, when we equip someone, we are giving them the tools and resources that are necessary to ensure they have a successful journey in life, at their job, and with their families. So, teaching and coaching by themselves are simply not enough. We must empower our team members by equipping them with the right tools and resources to do the job, accomplish the mission, and complete their goals.

By being coach-able and equipping their team members, leaders can create a culture of growth and development, where team members feel supported, empowered, and motivated to achieve their goals. Coach-able leaders are also more likely to lead by example, demonstrating a commitment to self-improvement and inspiring their team members to do the same.

Empowering Others by Paying Attention to Detail

I believe attention to detail isn't simply about meticulousness, like crossing your t's and dotting your i's. It transcends into the realm of caring for people around you, ensuring you're poised to assist them before turmoil ensues or when they are in trouble. This consideration extends into helping people navigate life and business safely to avoid potential pitfalls, or even better, coaching them to sidestep trouble altogether.

Before I share a story from my time in the military, I want to share with you a list of reasons why attention to detail is so important and why it is important to empower others to be coach-able leaders.

Here is the list of reasons why we need to pay attention to detail to be successful and significant in empowering others to be coach-able:

- Protects your credibility

- Improves your reputation

- Elicits trust

- Improves teamwork

- Elevates everyone through trust

- Improves timeliness and ability to get things done in a set time

- Enables you to honor your word or promise if made

- Increases productivity

- Decreases chance for misinterpretation

- Reduces errors

- Improves ability to plan more carefully

- Reduces questions of accuracy

- Stems from habits

- Leads to more-thorough communication

- Improves organizational skills

- Decreases distractions

- Allows you to learn from past mistakes

- Improves ability to focus on tasks

- And many, many more!

Let me share a story about my first experience with attention to detail in the military.

My time at Biloxi, Mississippi, when I was stationed at Keesler Air Force Base for communications-electronics officer training, particularly underlines this principle.

Our training lasted six months, twice the duration allocated to flight line officers, underscoring the technical and stringent requisites demanded to successfully navigate the communication–electronics officer curriculum.

I'd heard that, at least at the time, the base had the highest rate of suicide or attempted suicide across the military, perhaps due to the intense competition and pressure within the electronics-education domain. Here, we were tasked with equipping individuals to create electronic and circuit boards for a wide array of devices such as radar, radio, television, telephone, and the burgeoning field of computers.

In the midst of this demanding school and training environment, I volunteered for additional duties, particularly to be the director to coordinate the Special Olympics for Mississippi, Alabama, and Louisiana. My prior experiences in assisting with the Special Olympics in Minnesota and Wisconsin, coupled with work involving kids with disabilities in swimming and gymnastics, seemed to dovetail into this opportunity seamlessly. My role as the Special Olympics director demanded extensive coordination across the three states, challenging my organizational skills and execution ability to host a stellar event for the athletes with disabilities and have adapted.

After a rigorous interview process, I was promoted to the director position and had to report to the colonel's office for guidance and coaching on organizing the Special Olympics at Keesler Air Force Base. This significant responsibility demanded countless hours of training, coordination, and communication. Furthermore, most of the training was happening among very young, impressionable male and female airmen who had just graduated from basic training school.

On one occasion, as the colonel led me through a hall corridor, I noticed one of his back pockets was unbuttoned. In the military, this is one of the ways we teach and discipline others to pay attention to detail. All pockets on uniforms need to be buttoned. The gig line—the buttons on your shirt, the belt buckle, and the zipper on your pants—needs to be a straight line. During basic training, cadets and newbies are given demerits if they do not have a pocket buttoned or if the gig line is off. On this occasion, despite noting in my mind that this colonel's pocket was unbuttoned, I hesitated to inform him and chose instead to ignore it, thinking that it might help to avoid potentially embarrassing him.

However, just a short distance into our walk, a young airman diligently cleaning the floor on his hands and knees noticed the same pocket unbuttoned and alerted the colonel to his unbuttoned pocket. Graciously, the colonel thanked him, rectifying the minor yet perceptible oversight.

It seemed minor, yet upon our return, the colonel confronted me with a critical inquiry: Why hadn't I informed him about the unbuttoned pocket? Why had I allowed the young airman to catch this oversight instead of ensuring his impeccable appearance was maintained so he could be a good example for the airmen? I had actually embarrassed the colonel more so by not catching the open pocket before one of the basic airmen caught it. Hats off to the airman for his attention to detail and for holding the colonel responsible for his discipline.

His words struck me profoundly. I had seen the unbuttoned pocket but chose to remain silent, thinking it was a minor matter. But this scenario underscored a paramount lesson: attention to detail, however seemingly inconsequential, matters. This attention-to-detail practice could prevent a minor oversight from snowballing into a significant issue, potentially averting catastrophic outcomes.

From that incident, I gleaned the true depth of ensuring attention to detail—not only ensuring my tasks were executed with meticulousness but also safeguarding the presentation and performance of those around me that I was entrusted to respect and protect.

As you embark on working with your team, remember to pay attention to the finer details. Not merely in your actions but also in safeguarding and uplifting your teammates. In essence, keep a vigilant eye on those seemingly insignificant details, as they can have a profound impact on the broader mission and the collective team's accomplishments.

The best way to improve your attention-to-detail skills is to have others hold you accountable to check on your work. Many organizations have no formal quality control department that can serve that purpose, so asking three to five people to act as your accountability partner team will go a long way to allowing others to help you learn attention to detail. If you are not prior military, asking people who are retired veterans, active duty, guard, or reserve, or past veterans who could serve to be a part of your accountability team will also help you to put a plan in place to improve and grow your attention-to-detail skills.

Trike on!

3. Mentoring Team Members

Navigating Gray Areas While Staying Coach-able

In the world of coaching, whether you're the one coaching others or being coached, you'll sometimes encounter a gray area. It's a space where the boundaries of what can be adjusted or overlooked within a given rule or directive become a bit hazy or gray. I'd like to share a story that illustrates this and the intricate interplay between being coach-able and understanding when to question or navigate the rules flexibly.

Consider a high-level gymnast—we'll call him Barry—who specialized in power tumbling and trampoline. In one notable year, this athlete not only qualified for the national competition but also competed globally, earning a spot on the USA team for the Trampoline Gymnastics World Championships in Australia. That's a grand stage, representing the United States in a major international competition—a dream and honor for any athlete, right?

Now, here's the twist: Upon learning that this student was going to be missing school to attend the World Championships, the school principal intended to mark Barry with an unexcused absence for the duration of the competition, and a lot of confusion ensued. The principal's explanation to justify Barry's unexcused absence was that this World Championships was not an authorized school activity.

What was the justification for marking this student-athlete absent? The competition was not considered a school-sponsored activity, and therefore, the student-athlete would be marked absent. Pause and ponder that for a moment.

The school was willing to excuse absences for its activities but was unwilling to excuse an athlete representing not just their school, city, community, or state but the entire United States.

Determined to get the unexcused absence authorized, Barry's mother met with the principal. She sought to understand the principal's position: her son, representing the whole nation, was to be penalized with unexcused absences? That is what it looked like.

The principal stood firm and confirmed that the student would be marked absent. So Barry's mother presented an ultimatum and "coached" the principal to reconsider within three minutes, or she would withdraw all three of her children from the school, equating to a potential financial loss of about $24,000 for the school that year.

Suddenly, the discussion pivoted. An exception could be made, it seemed, when the "mother bear" put it like that. The athlete was excused and went on to represent the United States at the world championships, doing remarkably well.

Yet the pivotal lesson extended beyond the athletic competition and lay in understanding the essence of rules, regulations, and policies. Sometimes, leaders need to coach people in just plain common sense so they can comprehend the underlying purpose of a law or policy. That allows us to discern when the policy might be appropriately adapted, especially when, in this situation, this was only a school policy, not a law. For instance, representing your country on a world stage might warrant a justified deviation from a policy. Again, this situation only encompassed a school rule or policy and not a law. So why was the principal so adamant and unwilling to make an exception unless it had a negative effect on the school's budget? I will let you draw a conclusion, but this is a great example of caring for others with the heart and not simply leading with the head.

In this scenario, while the athlete was representing the United States, they were also indirectly representing their school. The principal's initial resistance, due to the event not being school sanctioned, missed this point. Thus, the bottom line draws us back to pondering our own coach-ability and understanding the spirit behind rules and policies.

Can you remain coach-able while also possessing an intuitive grasp on the deeper understanding and intent of rules and policies and knowing when they might be mindfully and respectfully bent or more appropriately considered excused for a good or higher purpose? In this instance, it was less about rigid adherence to a rule and more about understanding the broader picture with its relevant values, vision, and mission.

In conclusion, coach-ability is a critical trait for effective leadership. By being coach-able, leaders can use feedback effectively, empower and mentor team members, and create a culture of growth and development. Coach-able leaders are better equipped to lead by example, inspire their team members, and achieve their goals.

4. Servant Leadership

Character-Driven Coaching and My Journey with Coach Bud Schmidt

Back in high school, I had a remarkable coach named Bud Schmidt. Coach Bud wasn't just our swimming coach for competitive and recreational teams but also a mentor through his apprentice program.

Coach Bud taught me all about how to "serve and not de-serve." Did you catch that word, *de-serve*? That wasn't misspelled. When we are self-focused and not serving others first, we "de-serve" them and keep them from receiving everything we could add real value to them with. Coach Bud's program wasn't only about teaching us swimming and lifesaving techniques—it was about coaching us to coach others in these skills too. Bud was someone who gently tucked me under his wing, imparting not only the technical aspects of swimming but also crucial life skills like communication, teamwork, problem-solving, and critical thinking.

His teachings were deeply empathetic and inclusive, extending to adapting swimming techniques for people with disabilities—those who might be without an arm or a leg and desired to experience the joy of swimming. Coach Bud was focused on coaching leaders—and in his case, he used swimming as his vehicle to effectively build and grow coaches who, in turn, were going to grow up as *coach-leaders* themselves. I define *coach-leaders* as those leaders who are dedicated and passionate about coaching others to be leaders as well. Most companies do not have a formal coach-leader program, and they leave it up to chance, which generally does not bode well in the long run for the companies.

Few companies and organizations intentionally grow coach-leaders in their cultures. Most of the time, I think the C-level leadership in those companies simply expects that because someone is put in a position of leadership with responsibility, they will somehow intuitively know how to lead and will automatically be a leader. This couldn't be further from the truth. In day-to-day operations, if companies and their leadership were intentional about growing and developing coach-leaders, the cultures of those companies would be much more healthy, and the success of the company would be more long term.

We so desperately need coach-leaders in every organization, and more than ever we need the parents in the homes to be coach-leaders for their mates and for their children. Bud's approach to teaching us was compassionate and comprehensive. Whoever coached Coach Bud during his growth, their wisdom was now being generously passed down to us. He was comprehensive in helping us understand how to break down swimming skills and how to isolate those skills to train for strength and efficiency while teaching and coaching. In terms of being comprehensive, Bud showed us how to look at each swimming stroke with a very critical eye to correct the stroke with feedback. We even had a window below our pool where we could observe swimmers from underneath the water to more effectively scrutinize their strokes and techniques. This was in an era without recording equipment, so our eyes, keenly observing through that underwater window, were our best tool in analyzing and breaking down every swimming stroke.

He was compassionate because he treated each person fairly and equitably while remaining passionate about the sport and life skills of swimming. Later in this chapter, I will introduce you to Steve, who had no arms, so Bud taught us to adapt our teaching and coaching skills and make swimming enjoyable and possible for everyone.

Reflecting on the Tricycle Effect, the back two wheels symbolize competence. Bud was certainly instilling technical swimming competence in us, covering the intricate details of flutter kicking and different strokes, like crawl, butterfly, breaststroke, and more.

Yet he also embedded lessons of leadership and teamwork from the other competence wheel, the people skills wheel, in the realm of swimming, even if that team was just two people. Sometimes, the most potent team can be as small and fundamental as a husband and wife, gradually expanding with children, and crafting their family through their unique team and family dynamics.

As I shared earlier, Bud went far beyond the wheels of competence in the Tricycle Effect. He emphasized leading with character as well. I recall him working with a student named Steve, who didn't have arms but was eager to swim. Bud believed I could assist him, and he assigned Steve to my purview to teach him how to swim, dive, and survive in deep water for long periods of time.

Helping Steve with various tasks, from getting dressed to navigating through the pool, was a profoundly humbling and enlightening experience. I learned about caring for and acknowledging Steve's emotions, dreams, and goals, just like anyone else, thus learning to lead with character first in teaching and coaching my own swimming classes. I truly learned to serve others, coach others, and *not* focus on or think that I might deserve some award or accolades. It was my job to add value to others and, in doing so, bring success to my life and significance to those I coached. I recently learned that Steve works as a leader in the state government and has a healthy and happy family. Hopefully, in some small way, I like to think that my teaching and coaching helped prepare Steve with the leadership he has today with his family and occupation.

Bud was a coach who led more by example than by words, genuinely caring about all of his apprentices in the swimming coaching program. I am immensely grateful for Bud's willingness to pass on his tremendous coaching to me. This foundational experience guided me to become a water-safety instructor, following in Bud's footsteps. Over the years, I taught and lifeguarded thousands of pool activities and instructed hundreds of kids in lifesaving, swimming, and diving lessons.

So, whenever you find yourself coaching someone, serve them, and invest in them as Bud invested in me. Go beyond the technical and people skills and serve them the most by helping them develop their character. Ensure they not only become competent and skillful but also caring, trustworthy, respectful, fair, and empathetic.

Stay coach-able, my friend, and always trike on!

Chalk Talk Coaching Tip

Coach-ability in leadership fosters a culture where feedback becomes a catalyst for growth, driving leaders to be humble and practice humility as they lead by example and coach others to do the same. Embracing the role of a coach-leader, they not only guide personal and professional journeys but also craft a legacy of character-driven leadership that empowers others to achieve and exceed their own potential.

- **Promise of solution**: This chapter promises to equip leaders with the understanding and tools to leverage feedback for personal and team growth, ensuring they remain humble, open, and able to coach others toward shared success.

- **Suggested action item**: To implement this solution, leaders should commit to a regular feedback cycle with their teams, actively soliciting and providing constructive feedback, setting specific growth-oriented goals, and following up on progress. Leaders can start by scheduling monthly feedback sessions that include self-reflection and team reflection directly from their people to identify strengths, weaknesses, and opportunities for growth and development.

Workbook for Coach-Ability, Chapter 12

The Importance of Character in Leadership

Fill-in-the-Blanks

1. Being coach-able is an essential trait for effective leadership, including how to use feedback _____ and how to empower and mentor team members.

2. Leaders who are coach-able are more _____, open to feedback, and better equipped to use it to improve their performance.

3. Coach-able leaders are better equipped to lead by _____, inspire their team members, and achieve their goals.

Reflective Questions

1. Reflect on a time when you received feedback that was hard to accept. How did you use that feedback to

improve your leadership skills? What were the results of implementing this feedback?

2. Think about a leader you admire who embodies coach-ability. What specific actions or behaviors of this leader demonstrate their coach-ability, and how have these actions influenced your perception or actions as a leader?

3. Consider a situation where you had to coach someone else. How did you approach this, and what were the outcomes? What did this experience teach you about your own capacity for leadership and mentorship?

Summary of Chapter 12 Workbook

In chapter 12, the focus is on the integral role coach-ability plays in cultivating effective leadership. The chapter underlines the power of feedback as not just a tool for personal growth but as a breakfast of champions that strengthens leadership. It emphasizes the importance of humility in leaders, who must remain open to feedback to enhance their performance and facilitate the growth of others. The narrative supports the concept of leaders as coaches, who are not only responsible for guiding their personal and professional growth but also for nurturing and serving their people who will be their future leaders. The chapter encourages leaders to exemplify coach-ability by demonstrating a commitment to self-improvement, thus inspiring others to follow suit in their journey toward collective and individual achievements.

Part 4:

Others Coach Us — Examples in Real Life

CHAPTER 13
The Importance of Character in Leadership

Faith sees the invisible, believes the unbelievable, and receives the impossible. — Corrie ten Boom[87]

NAVIGATING THROUGH THE COMPLEXITIES of our digital world, we encounter a multifaceted issue: cyberbullying. It isn't restricted merely to offensive text messages. Cyberbullying pervades through online reviews, emails, and various message formats, providing a seemingly invisible platform for bullies to inflict harm without the immediate consequences they might face in a face-to-face interaction.

> **Challenge/Problem statement:** Cyberbullying presents a complex challenge in the digital age, inflicting invisible harm across various platforms without immediate consequences.

Through this chapter, I urge you to stand strong as a source of support in mentoring others. Through their life experiences based on their dreams, difficulties, failures, and successes, they sometimes are our best mentors. Help them reach their highest dreams, goals, and wishes by truly caring for them and giving them the bravery they need. And don't forget to allow them to mentor you, using their own knowledge and skills to guide you just like a coach does with their team.

Let me share a short story about a mom and daughter who were looking for a gymnastics club that was safe and served as a coach mentoring the athletes in both the sport and life.

I had no idea that I would learn so much from this mom and her daughter as a mentee (someone being mentored by others). They helped me understand how to care for cyberbullying victims. Here is the story.

One day, a ninth grader and her mother visited our gym. The young lady, let's call her Jennifer, was an aspiring level-eight gymnast (with level 10 being the highest level in gymnastics). She was seeking a nurturing environment to continue her athletic journey. My wife, Kathy, engaged with her in a testing session to determine her skill level. Meanwhile, I conversed with her mother and unearthed a painful reality.

Contrary to initial appearances, the mother was here not only to assess our facility and our coaching style and skill. She was interviewing us, because she also wanted to ensure we were a safe haven for her daughter and would make good coaches who could coach her daughter back to health and wholeness in gymnastics. Their previous experience in another gym was marred by persistent cyberbullying, not only from fellow athletes but also from her coach, which had significantly affected her daughter's emotional and physical well-being.

As weeks turned into months, Jennifer became part of our Deutsch gym family. Her minor physical injuries could be masked by tape on her ankles, wrists, and elbows, but her emotional scars from the cyberbullying were not as easy to mask from the emotional pain. Thus began a gradual healing and self-belief-building process.

Each week, she'd travel an hour to our gym, sometimes five days a week. During our sessions, as I taped up old physical injuries to her ankles and elbows, I'd gently inquire about her day and any cyberbullying encounters she might have had, assuring her that she was in a safe and caring space. Slowly, we coached her through overcoming the traumatic experiences, reestablishing her confidence, and nurturing her ability to stand up against cyberbullying through positive self-talk and our unwavering support.

Even though Jennifer never knew it, she was mentoring me as much as I was coaching and mentoring her. I learned a lot, and I have put that learning and experience into practice for our other gym daughters over the years since then.

Over the subsequent three years that Jennifer was in our gym, she blossomed in our care, rediscovering her love for gymnastics and regaining a trustful environment where she could practice fully, fail freely, and perform successfully. Her healing journey was as triumphant as any victorious gymnastic performance, symbolizing a deeper, emotional conquest.

When the time approached for her graduation, it was bittersweet for all of us. The mother, expressing her gratitude, penned a heartfelt letter to Kathy and me, acknowledging the profound impact of our coaching her daughter back to the joy she had for gymnastics and leading with character first in our coaching styles.

Here is the letter that the mom and dad wrote to Kathy and me at the end of those three years:

Brandy (Gym Mom) Testimonial

Deutsch's gymnastics has been a blessing for our daughter and our family. We've come to appreciate so many things during our time here.

Professionalism on many levels. They have the knowledge and experience to get gymnasts where they want to go. As we have personally found, this is not true of all gyms and coaches.

Dane and Kathy are very purposeful in how they run their gym. From the music they choose to play to their attention with the gymnasts' health and safety.

They have developed the culture of hard work and respect. These are valuable in and out of the gym. Meaningful conversations take place that have value in their content and add to the lives and the experiences of the girls. No gossip or backbiting from the top down.

The coaches model patience and perseverance—they encourage and correct. They are "injury aware," understanding a healthy body is needed for best performance. They are about the physical well-being of the gymnasts and can help to care for and allow time for healing for injuries. This also is not something found everywhere.

So many things to say! I don't know how to say it all.

But, thank you!

Bob and Brandy (proud gym dad and gym mom)

In my reflective moments since Jennifer left our gym, I realized that when character is prioritized in mentorship, the depth and quality of influence that can be exerted are incomparable. Children, especially, possess a keen ability to discern genuine care and concern, and as this young gymnast worked with us, she could palpably sense our sincere, unwavering support—not just for the athlete she was but for the person she was blossoming into.

So, I encourage you to be a beacon of unwavering support for those around you, and let them coach and mentor you as much as you might them. By genuinely caring for them and infusing them with the courage to realize their utmost desires, you can assist them in achieving their dreams, goals, and aspirations.

Continue to be humble and coach-able as a mentee, and don't forget to welcome coaching and mentoring from those around you.

Trike on!

Chalk Talk Coaching Tip

In chapter 13, the profound effect of reciprocal mentorship is emphasized, revealing how guiding others through their trials and triumphs enriches the mentor's understanding and compassion. This cycle of support and learning highlights that mentorship is a two-way street, where both mentor and mentee grow in character and leadership.

- **Promise of solution:** By providing a nurturing and supportive environment, leaders can empower and mentor individuals like Jennifer to overcome the emotional impact of cyberbullying, fostering resilience and positive self-talk.

- Suggested action step: To implement this solution, create a mentorship program that includes regular check-ins focused on emotional well-being, encourages open dialogue about cyberbullying experiences, and offers strategies for building self-esteem and coping with online harassment.

Workbook for Coach-Ability, Chapter 13

Fill-in-the-Blanks

1. To truly benefit from mentorship, it is crucial to approach it with _____, allowing yourself to be open to learning and growth through the experiences and wisdom of others.

2. A mentor is not just a teacher but a guiding figure who can help a mentee harness their potential and navigate through challenges with _____ and patience.

3. The journey of overcoming cyberbullying for Jennifer was marked by the consistent and _____ support that helped rebuild her confidence and joy in gymnastics.

Reflective Questions

1. Reflect on a time when displaying humility allowed you to learn something valuable from another person. How

did this experience change the way you view the role of a mentor or mentee in your life?

2. Think about the mentors in your life. How has their guidance shaped the person you are today, and in what ways can you emulate their approach to mentorship to benefit others?

3. Consider the character skill of humility in leadership. How can practicing humility enhance your ability to both provide and receive mentorship, and why is this exchange important for personal and professional development?

Summary of Chapter 13 Workbook

In this chapter, we explored the multifaceted challenges of a healing journey from cyberbullying and the profound impact of mentorship in overcoming such obstacles. The narrative demonstrated how humility and character-driven leadership play pivotal roles in effective mentorship, allowing individuals to learn and grow through mutual support and shared experiences. By embracing humility, we open ourselves up to the valuable lessons that mentors offer, and we also prepare ourselves to be better mentors to others. The story of Jennifer and her mother's experience with our gymnastics club illustrates the transformative power of a nurturing environment led by empathetic and character-focused coaches. This chapter serves as a reminder of the importance of being coach-able and the irreplaceable value of having mentors who lead with character and humility.

CHAPTER 14
Your Word Is Your Bond: A Lesson in Integrity and Commitment

> *Honesty and integrity are absolutely essential for success in life—all areas of life. The really good news is that anyone can develop both honesty and integrity.*
> — Zig Ziglar[88]

NOTICE THAT ZIG IS saying that honesty and integrity can be developed. That is so profound! As we have been sharing throughout this book, character can be developed, and character skills can be practiced, improved, and grown by anyone.

> **Challenge/Problem statement:** Upholding integrity and commitment can be challenging when facing conflicting orders or pressures in leadership roles.

To highlight the honesty and integrity character skills in a practical sense, let me assure you that as you are learning these skills, you will most likely be tested in life on what you learned and if you are truly committed to building character as a leader. Let me take you back to a pivotal moment in my life when these two character skills were put to the ultimate test, and I persevered. When I served as a captain, assigned as the chief of maintenance and accountable for all IT throughout Turkey, I was chosen by my boss, who previously worked as President Reagan's communications director, specifically for this role and to serve under him.

After completing a very important inspection of the whole group, my boss, the colonel, received the inspection results report but lacked the immediate time to review the details of its contents and put corrections into place. Before embarking on a 30-day vacation, he summoned me to his office. His request was precise: Safeguard the inspection report, ensuring no one else viewed it until his return. He emphasized this was a direct order. He said, "No one, but no one is to see that report." Well, after hearing his order, I assured him that I would keep the report confidential, and no one would be allowed to see it. I accepted his legal order and did not anticipate any significant difficulties at all.

Stowing the report in my locked desk drawer, I believed that would be the end of it until he returned from vacation. But sometimes, unexpected challenges in life seldom follow our expectations or planned scripts.

A few hours after the colonel's departure, the vice commander, now the acting authority and commander in the absence of the colonel, requested to see the report. Despite his being the current commander, his rank, and my respect for his authority, I couldn't comply due to the clear instructions and orders from the commander on vacation.

The vice commander pressed me really hard, offering a counterorder to produce the report, but I stood firm. I had given my word to the colonel, and I had received a legal order from the previous commander. Therefore, despite the major's threats of an Article 15 and a potential court-martial, I held my ground. Integrity, in this moment, was about upholding my first commitment, and to a legal order, even in the face of undesirable consequences.

As I soon learned, the major did start Article 15 proceedings to court-martial me, so for almost an entire month, I was sitting on pins and needles, thinking my military career was over.

The colonel's return a month later brought a surprising turn of events. Inquiring about the interim period, he was initially shocked to hear of my potential court-martial that had been started, but then he erupted into laughter. I did not see anything humorous about my situation, but from behind his desk, he produced a plaque, awarding me European Officer of the Year. Wow! I had no idea that he had even nominated me for that award. The colonel affirmed my actions in standing my ground were commendable, and he assured me that the court-martial would never materialize. True to his word, it did not.

The essence of this story pivots on a fundamental principle: Your word is your bond. Even if I had been court-martialed, adhering to my commitment to the colonel would have remained the right action. But where does your ethical compass point? Do you have a firm line in the sand that dictates your actions, even when challenged?

Occasionally, maintaining ethical and moral integrity may bring unforeseen consequences. When those circumstances come, and they most certainly will, regardless of the consequences, we must coach others through our character-driven leadership by example. Choosing to do the right thing, for the right reason, at the right time, stands paramount and is the *high road* to success and significance. It takes real courage, just like the seat in the Tricycle Effect highlights. As *high road leaders*, just as John C. Maxwell advises character-driven leaders in his book *High Road Leadership*, we choose courage on the path of character, even if it doesn't agree with everyone.[89]

> One of my colleagues, Dave Anderson, author of *Becoming a Leader of Character,* says, "Courage is the fulcrum of leadership."[3]

A handshake symbolized an unbreakable promise during my time in Turkey, particularly outside metropolitan zones like Izmir, Istanbul, and Ankara. A verbal commitment was considered as unyielding as any formal agreement. It's crucial for us to rediscover and uphold this simplicity and directness in our daily actions, so we are thoroughly committed to honesty and integrity in leadership. John C. Maxwell on his author page for his book *High Road Leadership* says, "Leaders who practice high road leadership value all people, do the right things for the right reasons, take accountability for their actions, and place people above their own agenda."[91]

In closing, team, I urge you to ensure your promises are not merely words but steadfast commitments. Let your word truly be your bond and coach others to do likewise.

As always, trike on!

Chalk Talk Coaching Tip

In the realm of character, staying true to your commitments is paramount, and this chapter underscores that with a real-life military example where integrity and a promise made were put to the test. Upholding your word, especially in times of pressure, exemplifies the core values and commitment to honesty and integrity, which are critical to both personal character and effective leadership.

- **Promise of solution:** By steadfastly adhering to their word and legal orders, leaders exemplify integrity, earning trust and respect even when facing adverse consequences.

- **Suggested action step**: Establish a personal code of ethics to guide decisions, ensuring alignment with your deepest values, and when faced with ethical dilemmas, consult this code to steer actions that uphold your commitments, regardless of external pressures.

Workbook for Coach-Ability, Chapter 14

Your Word Is Your Bond: A Lesson in Integrity and Commitment

Fill-in-the-Blanks

1. Even if I had been court-martialed, adhering to my commitment to the colonel would have remained the right action because your word is your _____.

2. The essence of this story pivots on a fundamental principle: your word is your _____, which is nonnegotiable in the realm of ethical leadership.

3. In Turkey, a handshake was more than a mere gesture. It symbolized an _____ promise, one that held as much weight as any formal contract.

Reflective Questions

1. Recall a time when you had to choose between an

easy way out and keeping a promise. How did you respond, and what did the outcome teach you about the importance of integrity?

2. Consider the last time you faced a moral dilemma where doing the right thing came with risks or potential personal loss. How did you navigate this situation, and how did it shape your understanding of commitment?

3. Reflect on your experiences with mentorship, either as a mentor or a mentee. How has humility played a role in these relationships, and can you identify a situation where the mentorship received or given was instrumental in overcoming a challenge?

Summary of Chapter 14 Workbook

In Chapter 14, titled "Your Word is Your Bond: A Lesson in Integrity and Commitment," we delve into the importance of honesty and integrity in leadership. The chapter begins with a profound quote from Zig Ziglar, emphasizing that honesty and integrity can be developed and are essential for success in all areas of life.

The author shares a personal story from his time as a captain in the military, highlighting a pivotal moment where his integrity was tested. After receiving a direct order from his superior to safeguard an inspection report and ensure no one else viewed it, he faced immense pressure from a vice commander who demanded access to the report. Despite the threats of court-martial and the potential end of his military career, the author stood firm in his commitment to his superior's orders.

This chapter illustrates the critical lesson that keeping one's word, even under difficult circumstances, is a testament to true character. It reinforces the idea that integrity should be the foundation of leadership, guiding decisions and actions. The author urges readers to make their promises steadfast commitments and to coach others to do the same, embodying high-character leadership and adding value to others' lives through character-driven actions.

CHAPTER 15
Cultivating Positive Mindsets Through Humility and Mentorship

We've explored the concepts of self-talk and self-coaching in this book.

> **Challenge/Problem statement:** Negative thinking often spreads more rapidly and pervasively than positive thinking, which can hinder personal and collective growth and well-being.

I recall an intriguing podcast episode hosted by Lewis Howes, a *New York Times* best-selling author, two-time All-American athlete, keynote speaker, and entrepreneur. He runs a program called *The School of Greatness*. During one YouTube episode, an essential question was raised: which is more critical, positive thinking or reducing negative thinking?[92]

The answer was that diminishing negative thinking is more potent and crucial than mere positive thinking.[93] This reminds me of the social media realm, where a negative post circulates seven times faster and garners more engagement than a positive one.[94]

It's somewhat disheartening, isn't it? A negative post zips around the world at a speed much faster than a positive one.[95] Even good news travels fast, but bad news travels faster. It feels as if it should be the opposite, but human brains and interests don't naturally lean that way. People often focus more on negativity at face value rather than on positivity.[96] Research studies have shown that even false news, including lies, spreads faster than the truth.[97]

So, with so much negativity bias, it is even more important that we coach others to reduce negative thinking, stay positive, and spread positivity.[98]

This poses an essential point: Negative thinking, even a single negative thought, can potentially outweigh a positive one. Therefore, if we minimize negative thinking, our internal dialogue may inherently become more positive than if we solely attempt to think positively. Also, reigning in negative thinking may be somewhat simpler.

The emphasis is to have a good attitude and stay positive when coaching others. I have to constantly remind myself that out of over 40 team gymnasts, not all of them are going to have good days all the time. I may be the only shining light in their day sometimes, and it is up to me to coach them to enjoy their sport, their team, their coaches, and their art in gymnastics.

As the Bible suggests, we must take every thought captive. A verse from Second Corinthians 10 tells us: "We demolish arguments and every pretension that sets itself up against the knowledge of God, and we take captive every thought to make it obedient to Christ."[99] Indeed, by consciously capturing and counteracting negative thoughts, we practice less negative thinking.

In the gym, for the kids, I dub these pessimistic thoughts monkeys. These monkeys can plant fear and doubt in their little minds quickly enough, whispering things like *Isn't that scary?* or *You can't do that.*

Often, I advise them to instruct the monkeys to leave when they invade their thoughts. Essentially, this practice disrupts the negative-thinking process and halts the internal negative dialogue we all occasionally engage in.

While positive self-talk is beneficial, staunchly halting negative thoughts in their tracks may result in being more effective, steering us toward a positive mindset. So, remember: when you influence and coach yourself, you are also mentoring, coaching, and influencing others, and you may just be one decision away from success or failure.

Ensure you tell those monkeys (those negative thoughts) to go away and halt them in their tracks. As a result, you'll likely advance further, cultivating a more positive end result. In doing so, you coach not only yourself to success but also coach and guide others toward significance as well by helping them emulate the same.

No monkeys in the mind! Trike on!

Chalk Talk Coaching Tip

In the face of the constant negativity bias, our word becomes our steadfast commitment to uphold honesty and integrity, countering the rampant spread of negative thinking. By consciously eliminating negative self-talk, we honor our bond to ourselves and others, cultivating a mindset grounded in positivity and ethical action.

- **Promise of solution:** By actively minimizing negative thinking and fostering a positive internal dialogue, we promise to cultivate a more optimistic mindset that radiates positivity and improves mental resilience.

- Suggested action step: To implement this solution, practice daily thought audits where you consciously recognize negative thoughts as they arise, label them as unhelpful, and replace them with a constructive or positive statement. Over time, this will train your brain to default to a more positive outlook and reduce the frequency and impact of negative thoughts. Additionally, sharing this technique within your network can multiply its beneficial effects.

Workbook for Coach-Ability, Chapter 15

Cultivating Positive Mindsets Through Humility and Mentorship

Fill-in-the-Blanks

1. It's crucial to combat the brain's _____ bias by consciously choosing positivity over negativity.

2. To maintain a healthy attitude in the face of challenges, you must manage your inner _____ that spreads doubt and fear.

3. The act of capturing every negative thought aligns with the biblical teaching of making thoughts obedient to _____, fostering a disciplined mindset.

Reflective Questions

1. Reflect on a time when your humility helped turn a negative situation into a positive outcome. How did your approach

influence not only your mindset but also the attitudes of those around you?

2. Consider a mentor who has significantly influenced your life. What qualities did they possess that made their guidance effective, and how can you emulate those traits in your interactions with others?

3. Think about the concept of monkeys as negative thoughts. How can the practice of dismissing these monkeys lead to greater mental resilience and set a positive example for those you mentor?

Summary of Chapter 15 Workbook

In chapter 15, we explore the power of positive thinking and the importance of minimizing negative self-talk. The chapter encourages readers to be vigilant gatekeepers of their own minds, using the metaphor of monkeys to represent negative thoughts that must be actively dismissed. By doing so, we not only improve our own well-being but also set a positive example for those we mentor. This workbook aims to reinforce the concepts discussed in the chapter by providing exercises that promote reflection on humility, mentorship, and the cultivation of a positive mindset.

CHAPTER 16

Pressure Always Reveals True Character, and Then We Can Be Mentored

Pressure always reveals our true character, and then we can be mentored. — Dane A. Deutsch

I HAVE ALREADY SHARED with you my experience in climbing up Mt. Ararat, I know, but I want to recap that experience and share with you another coaching tip on how to most effectively allow others to coach and mentor us.

> **Challenge/Problem statement:** In life's ascent, whether literal mountains or metaphorical challenges, an individual's true character is revealed, and it's often under pressure that we must adapt and mentor one another through adversity.

Climbing Mt. Ararat was an amazing, once-in-a-lifetime experience. There were so many great life lessons learned in the few days we spent climbing together as a team. Remember, there were more than a dozen of us, lured by Turkish advertisements describing it merely as a tough hike. They even showed a green path up the mountain in one of their flyers. Whether it was photoshopped or not, we'll never know. But let me remind you, it was far more than a hike. It was a technical climb, and although we had crampons and ice picks, none of us were truly prepared for it.

We met the astronaut James Irwin, faced many risks and threats, and learned about altitude sickness and hypothermia. Perhaps most importantly, we also learned about ourselves, teamwork, and each team member's character.

Throughout this ordeal, I learned a pivotal lesson about human character: as you ascend in altitude, true personalities are unveiled and revealed.

People often say that sports build character. Well, I don't believe that. Just like with gymnastics being a vehicle for us as a sport, I believe that sports reveal your character and then we can build and coach it from there. Likewise, high altitude with physical pressure and lack of oxygen brings out the real character of each individual. Then you have to coach it and deal with it from there.

> "Sports don't build character. They reveal it." – Coach John Wooden/Jeywood Hale Broun

Many, including myself, had to coach, encourage, and physically assist teammates during each segment of the climb to the peak, some of whom were teetering between consciousness and unconsciousness, just to keep moving.

Conversely, we discovered the higher we went in altitude that we had a lone wolf in our group. His single-minded goal was to be the first to reach the top, and he did. Yet, he shared no communication or camaraderie with the rest of us. He slept in his own tent and remained emotionally and physically distant throughout the journey.

Life is akin to this treacherous climb. We're all bound to face some steep slopes, whether it be health issues, financial strife, or other life challenges. In addition, we will all be faced with working for a common goal with someone else who we find out is arrogant, self-centered, and selfish. They'll keep us from enjoying the journey but may also put us at risk as well. Keep this in mind because you never know—maybe you're the beacon of hope in supporting someone else who needs you to mentor and coach them during their uphill battle.

While it's one thing to be successful (like reaching the peak first), it's entirely another to be significant in adding value to others, aiding others in their quest for a goal and maybe even survival. During our climb, some team members chose empathy and sacrifice, opting not to reach the peak so they could assist the woman who was battling altitude sickness and ensure her safety and survival.

Mentoring, coaching, and coach-ability underscore this entire narrative. The lone wolf, whose sole ambition was to be the first to ascend, was uncoach-able. But the majority of our team embodied coach-ability, displaying a willingness to look out for one another, to mentor and coach each other physically for the climb, emotionally to keep going, and spiritually in prayer for each other.

When you pick your teammates in life, pick them wisely and treat them with the Golden Rule.

> John C. Maxwell says, "Those closest to you determine your level of success."[1]

Not everyone will have your back. But remember, you can be different because of your character skills. You can choose to be a person of character and lead by example, helping mentor others and allowing them to mentor you so that you can move beyond success to significance, embodying the Tricycle Effect.

Trike on!

Chalk Talk Coaching Tip

In the journey of personal growth and teamwork on treacherous paths in life like those of Mt. Ararat, our true commitment to character, such as humility, caring, and empathy, becomes apparent—not just in reaching the summit with the team but in the willingness to support and be mentored by others. The essence of being coach-able is not just about leading a team or ascending alone but about valuing the bonds of trust formed through mutual mentorship and the collective climb, showcasing our integrity in action and the character we reveal through our practical actions in life experiences.

- **Promise of solution:** By recognizing that adversity reveals character, we promise to leverage these moments as opportunities for growth and mentorship, transforming potential setbacks into valuable lessons of resilience and support.

- **Suggested action step**: Actively seek out challenging situations that test character, such as team-building exercises or difficult projects, and use these as opportunities to observe, reflect, and coach both yourself and others. Offer support when teammates struggle, and invite feedback to cultivate a culture of mutual mentorship and character development. Always remember that the journey is as important as the destination, and the way you handle the climb can inspire and elevate those around you.

Workbook for Coach-Ability, Chapter 16

Pressure Always Reveals True Character, and Then We Can Be Mentored

Fill-in-the-Blanks

1. As we ascended Mt. Ararat, the challenges we faced _____ our true character, revealing the importance of humility and the willingness to be mentored by other team members.

2. The lone wolf in our group exemplified the opposite of _____, focusing solely on his own goals rather than the team's collective success or the willingness to mentor others and to be mentored by others.

3. True success on our climb wasn't measured by being the first to reach the summit, but by showing _____ and caring for teammates who needed mentorship and support.

Reflective Questions

1. Recall a time when you faced a difficult challenge. How did it reveal your character, and in what ways did you demonstrate humility and the ability to learn from others?

2. Think about a situation where you might have acted as a lone wolf. How could you have engaged in mentorship to not only enhance your own experience but also contribute to the group's well-being?

3. Reflect on an achievement you are proud of. How did the guidance and support of others contribute to this success, and how did you pass on what you learned to mentor others?

Summary for Chapter 16 Workbook

Chapter 16 underscores the essence of character, particularly humility and mentorship, through the real-life experience of a treacherous climb up Mt. Ararat. It teaches us that while personal achievements are significant, the true measure of success lies in our ability to work with others, learn from their experiences, and offer guidance and mentorship, even in the midst of life-threatening circumstances. This chapter invites us to reflect on our interactions with others, encouraging us to build character through challenges and become better mentors and mentees (learners mentored by others) in our journey called life.

Conclusion

COACH-ABILITY IS AN ESSENTIAL trait for personal and professional growth. In *Coach-Ability and the Tricycle Effect*, we have discussed the definition of coach-ability, the signs of coach-ability, the benefits of coach-ability, how to develop coach-ability, barriers to coach-ability, how to overcome barriers to coach-ability, coaching, and mentorship for developing coach-ability, and how to encourage coach-ability in others.

> **Final challenge/problem statement:** Developing coach-ability often faces resistance due to fear of failure and a fixed mindset, which can hinder personal and professional growth.

Coach-ability is also the ability to be open to feedback, learn from experiences, and make positive changes to achieve personal and professional growth. Signs of coach-ability include active listening, willingness to learn and try new things, open-mindedness, self-awareness, responsibility, and accountability. The benefits of coach-ability include faster personal and professional growth, improved relationships with others, higher job satisfaction and career success, improved leadership skills, and better mentoring abilities.

To develop coach-ability, individuals can set learning goals, seek feedback, embrace a growth mindset, develop resilience and adaptability, and practice patience and persistence. Barriers to coach-ability include fear of failure, resistance to change, lack of self-awareness, lack of accountability, and a fixed mindset. To overcome these barriers, individuals can engage in self-reflection and awareness, seek support and guidance, challenge limiting beliefs, embrace a growth mindset, and take small steps toward change.

Coaching and mentorship are also essential for developing coach-ability. Effective coaching and mentorship practices involve establishing clear goals, providing constructive feedback, and offering support and guidance. Creating a supportive and safe environment for feedback and growth and developing strong relationships with coaches and mentors are also essential.

Finally, encouraging coach-ability in others and practicing coach-ability in leadership are critical for personal and organizational growth. By being coach-able, individuals can achieve their goals, unlock their full potential, and make a positive impact in their personal and professional lives.

In conclusion, developing coach-ability is a lifelong journey that requires dedication, perseverance, and a commitment to the growth and development of character-istics or character skills so we can be successful in adding value(s) to ourselves and significant by adding value(s) to others.

We encourage you to continue developing your character skills by remaining coach-able, being kind in coaching yourself, and

CONCLUSION

seeking out opportunities for learning and growth by adding value through coaching others. Also be sure to be open to feedback and constructive criticism through the influence of mentoring and coaching by others. By doing so, you can achieve your goals, unlock your full potential, and make a positive impact in the world. Success and significance can both coexist when we learn coach-ability by leading with character first with the Tricycle Effect!

Thank you for the privilege and honor to trek and trike with you and be your coach throughout this book journey.

Stay coach-able, my friend.

Trike on!

Coach Dane

- **Final promise of solution:** Committing to lifelong learning and self-improvement will break down the barriers to coach-ability, foster a growth mindset, and enhance adaptability, responsibility, and accountability.

- **Final** suggested action step: Implement the solution. Start a coach-ability journal where you record feedback received, reflect on it, set personal learning goals, and note down the steps you take each day toward growth. Regularly review and adjust your goals to ensure continued progress and embrace challenges as opportunities for learning.

Epilogue

CONGRATULATIONS ON REACHING THE end of this book, and what a journey it has been! Together, we've explored the depths of coach-ability, a path that I firmly believe is a lifelong one, filled with learning, growth, and endless opportunities for self-improvement. I poured my heart into these pages, hoping to inspire and guide you toward becoming more coach-able and unlocking greater successes in both your personal and professional life.

As we close this chapter, I want you to remember that becoming more coach-able isn't just a goal—it's a continuous journey. It's about embracing a growth mindset, being open to feedback, learning from every experience, and making those small but significant changes in your life. The tips, strategies, and insights in this book are just the beginning. They are the seeds planted to inspire and motivate you to keep growing and to move from mere success to true significance to reach peak performance.

Dane with his ice pick and crampons and a miniature model of Noah's Ark at the Peak on Mt. Ararat.

Developing coach-ability requires practice, patience, and persistence. It's not always easy, but the rewards are immeasurable. You're not just improving yourself—you're setting a foundation to make a positive impact in every aspect of your life as well as those of others.

If you're eager to continue this journey and want more guidance, I'm here to help. Visit my website at https://www.thetricycleeffect.com, and let's take the next step together. Click on the coaching section, and let's dive deeper into your personal growth and your company or organization's professional growth.

I wish you the very best on your life's journey. May you achieve success and significance, and may you always lead with character first. Keep growing, keep learning, and always be coach-able. You've got this!

Trike on!
Coach Dane

Coach-Ability Workbook Chapter Fill-in-the-Blanks Answer Key

Answers to Chapter 1 Fill-in-the-Blanks

1. "Leadership is **influence**, nothing more, nothing less." — John C. Maxwell

2. The triad of coach-ability consists of coaching **self**, coaching others, and being coached by others.

3. Being coach-able means aspiring to be a better leader, influencing ourselves through our own voices, pictures, dreams, goals, and **desires**.

Answers to Chapter 2 Fill-in-the-Blanks

1. The front wheel of the tricycle, dubbed the character skills wheel, includes spokes that are values and character-istics such as trustworthiness, respect, and **kindness**.

2. The two smaller rear wheels, known as the competence

skills wheels, represent the technical skills and **people** skills wheels, respectively.

3. Sitting atop the tricycle is the seat of **courage**, which represents the courage to make the right choices and decisions.

Answers to Chapter 3 Fill-in-the-Blanks

1. Coach-ability is the ability to be open to **feedback**, learn from experiences, and make positive changes to achieve personal and professional growth.

2. Being coach-able means having a growth mindset in all three ways of the coach-ability triad: **self**, others, and by others.

3. Coach-ability is important because it helps us **adapt** to new challenges and improve our outcomes and success.

Answers to Chapter 4 Fill-in-the-Blanks

1. Coach-ability is not just about being open to feedback. It's about being willing to learn and possessing character skills like **humility**, **vulnerability**, and loyalty.

2. Being coach-able involves traits such as active listening, willingness to learn and try new things, and **open-mindedness**.

3. The ability to be coach-able is the *key* to a more successful and **significant** life.

Answers to Chapter 5 Fill-in-the-Blanks

1. Coach-ability can help individuals develop a growth mindset, which can help them overcome obstacles, achieve their goals more quickly, and improve their **leadership** skills.

2. By being open to feedback and constructive criticism, individuals can improve their ability to listen actively and **communicate** effectively.

3. John C. Maxwell highlights that character is the **foundation** of leadership, showing its foundational role in effective leadership.

Answers to Chapter 6 Fill-in-the-Blanks

1. Principles like gravity or centrifugal force are outside of our body and outside our control, whereas **values** comprise our values internally.

2. When discussing character values, it is important to note that both **integrity** and **loyalty** play significant roles in leadership.

3. Being coach-able means first being coach-able and loyal by

influencing ourselves through our own **voices, pictures, dreams, goals,** and **desires.**

Answers to Chapter 7 Fill-in-the-Blanks

1. Fear of failure is one of the most common barriers to coach-ability, and overcoming it requires being intentional and developing a **growth** mindset.

2. When we discuss traditions and their importance in coaching character, we understand that these practices are not just about going through the motions, but they are meant to communicate deeper values of **honor, respect, trust,** and **protection.**

3. Overcoming resistance to change can be a significant barrier to coach-ability, and it requires developing a growth mindset, being open to new **ideas,** and being willing to take calculated **risks.**

Answers to Chapter 8 Fill-in-the-Blanks

1. By reflecting on their behaviors and actions, individuals can identify areas for improvement and develop **self-awareness.**

2. The RED Team is responsible for building the war scenario, throwing quarter sticks of dynamite and smoke grenades, as well as simulation-based injuries with people

to stage scenarios that are as **real** as possible.

3. No matter the rank, position, or authority, **debriefs** are very important for growth and learning from experiences.

Answers to Chapter 9 Fill-in-the-Blanks

1. Being open to **feedback** and constructive criticism can help individuals gain self-awareness and make positive changes to their behaviors and actions.

2. Coach-ability can lead to personal growth by helping individuals set **goals** and develop new skills and strategies.

3. Developing a **growth** mindset can help individuals overcome obstacles and setbacks and achieve their goals.

Answers to Chapter 10 Fill-in-the-Blanks

1. Effective coaching and mentorship practices are essential for developing **coach-ability**. These practices involve establishing clear goals, providing constructive feedback, and offering support and guidance.

2. A strong relationship with a coach or mentor can provide a **supportive** and safe environment, encouraging open communication and growth.

3. One essential character skill and a quality of effective

coaches and mentors is **humility**, which can help individuals navigate through personal and professional growth.

Answers to Chapter 11 Fill-in-the-Blanks

1. Creating a positive and encouraging environment is essential for coach-ability, which involves being kind, positive, **optimistic**, and supportive of others.

2. Leaders should provide opportunities for growth and **development**, offer constructive feedback, and recognize team members' efforts.

3. In fostering coach-ability, recognizing and celebrating **progress** and small wins are as important as acknowledging big victories.

Answers to Chapter 12 Fill-in-the-Blanks

1. Being coach-able is an essential trait for effective leadership, including how to use feedback **effectively** and how to empower and mentor team members.

2. Leaders who are coach-able are more **humble**, open to feedback, and better equipped to use it to improve their performance.

3. Coach-able leaders are better equipped to lead by

example, inspire their team members, and achieve their goals.

Answers to Chapter 13 Fill-in-the-Blanks

1. To truly benefit from mentorship, it is crucial to approach it with **humility**, allowing yourself to be open to learning and growth through the experiences and wisdom of others.

2. A mentor is not just a teacher but a guiding figure who can help a mentee harness their potential and navigate through challenges with **compassion** and patience.

3. The journey of overcoming cyberbullying for Jennifer was marked by the consistent and **empathetic** support that helped rebuild her confidence and joy in gymnastics.

Answers to Chapter 14 Fill-in-the-Blanks

1. Even if I had been court-martialed, adhering to my commitment to the colonel would have remained the right action because your word is your **bond**.

2. The essence of this story pivots on a fundamental principle: your word is your **bond**, which is nonnegotiable in the realm of ethical leadership.

3. In Turkey, a handshake was more than a mere gesture;

it symbolized an **unbreakable** promise, one that held as much weight as any formal contract.

Answers to Chapter 15 Fill-in-the-Blanks

1. It's crucial to combat the brain's **negativity** bias by consciously choosing positivity over negativity.

2. To maintain a healthy attitude in the face of challenges, you must manage your inner **dialogue** that spreads doubt and fear.

3. The act of capturing every negative thought aligns with the biblical teaching of making thoughts obedient to **Christ**, fostering a disciplined mindset.

Answers to Chapter 16 Fill-in-the-Blanks

1. As we ascended Mt. Ararat, the challenges we faced **revealed** our true character, revealing the importance of humility and the willingness to be mentored by other team members.

2. The lone wolf in our group exemplified the opposite of **coach-ability**, focusing solely on his own goals rather than the team's collective success or the willingness to mentor others and to be mentored by others.

3. True success on our climb wasn't measured by being the first to reach the summit but by showing **humility** and caring for teammates who needed mentorship and support.

Tricycle Effect Framework

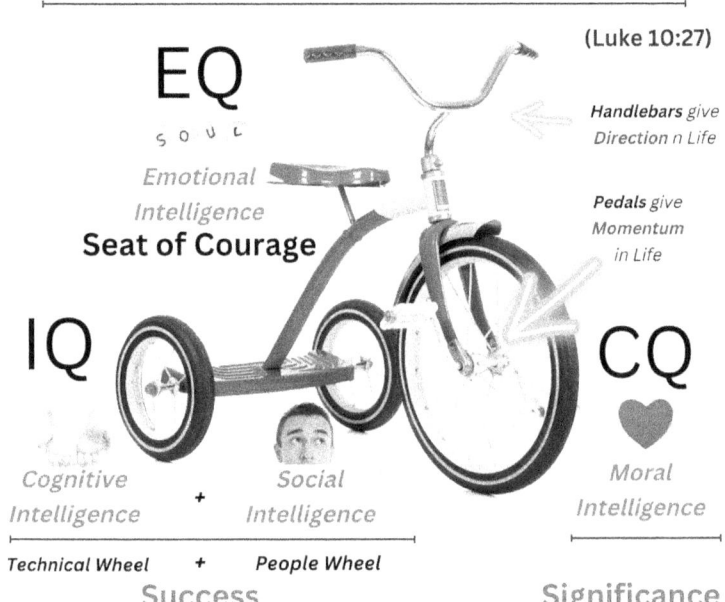

Tricycle Effect Wheels Worksheet

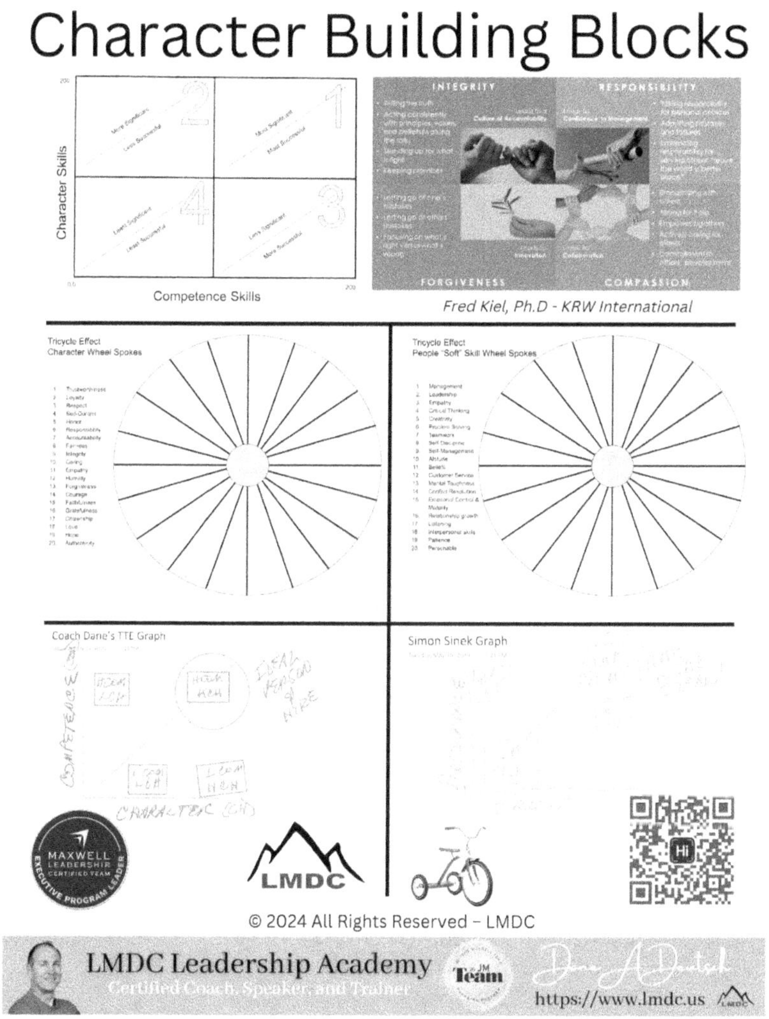

Character Building Blocks

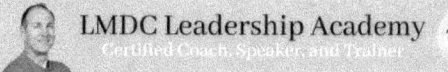

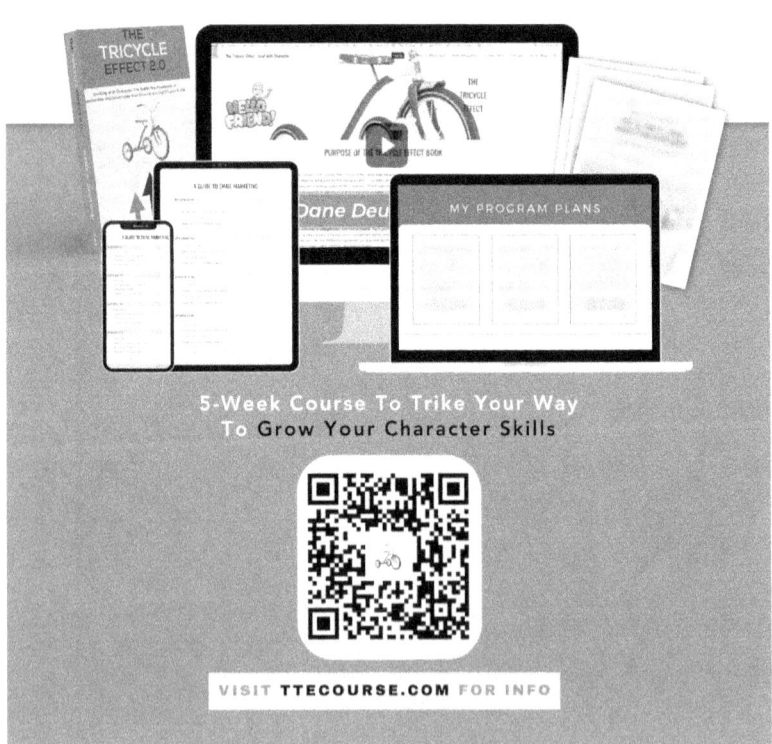

Resource and Reference List

Acuff, Jon. *Soundtracks: The Surprising Solution to Overthinking*. Ada, MI: Baker Books, 2021.

Anderson, Dave. "Courage and Defeating Your Fears," *Leader of Character*. April 15, 2024. Vimeo video, 1:11. https://vimeo.com/934950434.

Berkun, Scott. "How Skunkworks Got Its Name." Scott Berkun. July 13, 2006. https://scottberkun.com/2006/how-skunkworks-got-its-name-2.

Carlson, Chuck. *Game of My Life: 25 Stories of Packers Football*. Champaign, IL: Sports Publishing LLC, 2004.

Caspi, Avshalom. "Three-Year-Old's Traits Predict Personality at Age 26." *Journal of Personality* 71, no. 4 (2003): 496–513. https://education-consumers.org/briefpdfs/4.7-childrens_behavior_age_3.pdf.

Cherry, Kendra. "What Is the Negativity Bias?" Verywell Mind. Last updated November 13, 2023. https://www.verywellmind.com/negative-bias-4589618.

Collins, Jim. "BHAG." Jim Collins. Accessed May 12, 2024. https://www.jimcollins.com/concepts/bhag.html.

Covey, Stephen R. *The 7 Habits of Highly Effective People: Powerful Lessons in Personal Change.* New York: Free Press, 2004.

Covey, Stephen R., and Rebecca R. Merrill. *The Speed of Trust: The One Thing That Changes Everything.* New York: Free Press, 2018.

Deane, Michael T. "Top Six Reasons New Businesses Fail." Investopedia. Last updated April 1, 2024. https://www.investopedia.com/financial-edge/1010/top-6-reasons-new-businesses-fail.aspx.

Deutsch, Dane Andrew. *The Tricycle Effect: How to Be More Productive and Live a Successful and Significant Life by Leading with Character First.* Deutsch's Inc., 2016.

Duhigg, Charles. *The Power of Habit: Why We Do What We Do in Life and Business*, 10th anniversary ed. New York: Random House, 2023.

Ford, Henry. "Quote Page." *Reader's Digest.* September 1947.

Friend, Tad. "Jumpers." *New Yorker,* October 6, 2003, .

Gallo, Carmine. "Four Communication Lessons I Learned from Real Top Gun Fighter Pilots." *Inc.*, May 25, 2022, .

Gawdat, Mo. "Mo Gawdat: AI Today, Tomorrow and How You Can Save Our World (Nordic Business Forum 2023)." *Slo Mo with Mo Gawdat.* October 2, 2023. YouTube video, 29:04.

Howes, Lewis. "Do This to Cut Out Negativity from Your Life | Price Pritchett." Greatness Clips—Lewis Howes. November 30, 2023. YouTube video, 10:19. .

Gutman, Ron. "The Hidden Power of Smiling | Ron Gutman." TED. May 11, 2011. YouTube video, 7:26. https://www.youtube.com/watch?v=U9cGdRNMdQQ.

HeartMath Institute. "The Fascinating Relationship Between the Heart and Brain." November 21, 2021. YouTube video, 3:38. .

HeartMath Institute. "The 'Little Brain in the Heart.'" Accessed May 5, 2024.

Hepburn, Eric. "The Seven Times Distortion: Negativity Bias Reconsidered." Medium. June 14, 2023. https://ericdhepburn.medium.com/the-7x-distortion-negativity-bias-reconsidered-2456ab56e677.

Hornik, Jacob, Rinat Shaanan Satchi, Ludovica Cesareo, and Alberto Pastore. "Information Dissemination Via Electronic Word-Of-Mouth: Good News Travels Fast, Bad News Travels Faster!" *Computers in Human Behavior* 45 (2015): 273–280. .

"The Impact of Negative Thoughts and How to Process Them." The Waltline Group. Last updated June 11, 2020.

Javed, Saman. "Negative Social Media Posts Get Twice as Much Engagement Than Positive Ones, Study Finds." *Independent.* June 22, 2021. .

Jayakumar, Kripa. "One Smile Could Have Saved Him." Medium. May 20, 2020.

Jones, Laurie Beth. *Jesus, CEO: Using Ancient Wisdom for Visionary Leadership.* Westport, CT: Hyperion, 1996.

Kiel, Fred. *Return on Character: The Real Reason Leaders and Their Companies Win.* Boston: Harvard Business Review Press, 2015.

Kneller, James. "Can a Heart Transplant Change Your Personality?" JamesKnellerMD. July 14, 2021. YouTube video, 9:14. .

"KRW Return on Character, Marketing ROC, Study Guide #4." Lanesboro, MN: KRW International, 2021.

"KRW Return on Character, What Is Character, Study Guide #1." Lanesboro, MN: KRW International, 2021.

Leak, Ryan. *Chasing Failure: How Falling Short Sets You Up for Success.* Nashville, TN: W Publishing, 2021.

Linder, Jason. "Hacking the Brain's Negative Bias." *Mindfulness Insights* (blog). *Psychology Today.* May 8, 2021, .

Maltz, Maxwell. *Psycho-Cybernetics.* New York: Simon & Schuster, 1960.

Maxwell, John C. "Add Value to People." 12Stone Church. January 27, 2016. YouTube video, 2:24. .

Maxwell, John C. *Developing the Leader Within You.* New York: Thomas Nelson, 2005.

Maxwell, John C. *Ethics 101: What Every Leader Needs to Know.* 101 Series. New York: Center Street, 2008.

Maxwell, John C. *High Road Leadership: Bringing People Together in a World That Divides* Nashville, TN: Maxwell Leadership Publishing, 2024.

Maxwell, John C. *Sometimes You Win, Sometimes You Learn: Life's Greatest Lessons Are Gained from Our Losses.* New York: Center Street, 2015.

Maxwell, John C. *Success 101: What Every Leader Should Know.* New York: HarperCollins Leadership, 2008.

Maxwell, John C. *The 21 Irrefutable Laws of Leadership: Follow Them and People Will Follow You.* New York: HarperCollins Leadership, 2022.

Maxwell, John C. *There's No Such Thing as "Business" Ethics: There's Only One Rule for Making Decisions.* New York: Center Street Publishing, 2003.

Mehl, Matthias R., Simine Vazire, Nairán Ramírez-Esparza, Richard B. Slatcher, and James W. Pennebaker. "Are Women Really More Talkative Than Men?" *Science* 317, no. 5834 (2007): 82. .

Miller, Justin Thomas. "The Butterfly Effect: How Small Changes Lead to Big Progress." Justin Thomas Miller. Accessed May 5, 2024.

Munroe, Myles. *Power of Character in Leadership: How Values, Morals, Ethics, and Principles Affect Leaders.* New Kensington: Whitaker House, 2017.

Nader Remi, " 'Cellular Memory' Heart Transplant Recipient and a Neurosurgeon Interview," Webivores. February 20, 2018. YouTube video, 9:08.

Pagan, Eben. *The Client-Getting Script: 11 Proven Words to Turn a Conversation Into a High-Paying Client.* Self-published, 2023.

Pinocchio. Directed by Norman Ferguson. 1940; Burbank, CA: Walt Disney Productions, 1940.

Reagan, Ronald. "Remarks in Chicago, Illinois, at the Annual Convention and Centennial Observance of the United Brotherhood of Carpenters and Joiners." Speech, Chicago, IL, September 3, 1981. The American Presidency Project. Accessed July 16, 2024.

Sirk, Christopher. "Xerox PARC and the Origins of Gui." CRM.org. Last updated January 23, 2024. .

"Six Pillars of Character." Character Counts. Accessed May 12, 2024. .

"Suffering from Imposter Syndrome? The Cure May Be Growth Mindset." March 18, 2021. NeuroLeadership Institute. .

Tichy, Noel M., and Warren G. Bennis. *Judgment: How Winning Leaders Make Great Calls*. New York: Penguin Publishing, 2009.

Vosoughi, Soroush, Deb Roy, and Sinan Aral. "The Spread of True and False News Online." *Science* 359, no. 6380 (2018): 1146–1151. .

Wrigley, Patrick. "A Mystery on the Mountain of Pain." Roads and Kingdoms. November 25, 2014.

Ziglar, Tom. *Choose to Win: Transform Your Life, One Simple Choice at a Time.* Nashville, TN: Nelson Books, 2021.

Ziglar, Zig. *See You at the Top: 25th Anniversary Edition*. New Orleans: Pelican Publishing, 2000.

Endnotes

1. John C. Maxwell, *The 21 Irrefutable Laws of Leadership: Follow Them and People Will Follow You*, 25th anniversary edition (New York: HarperCollins Leadership, 2022), 4.

2. Matthias R. Mehl et al., "Are Women Really More Talkative Than Men?," *Science* 317, no. 5834 (2007): 82, https://doi.org/10.1126/science.1139940.

3. Maxwell, *The 21 Irrefutable Laws of Leadership*, 4.

4. Dane Deutsch, *The Tricycle Effect: How to Be More Productive and Live a Successful and Significant Life by Leading with Character First* (Deutsch's Inc., 2016), 32.

5. Billy Graham (@BillyGraham), "Integrity is the glue that holds our way of life together. Do you have it? #devotion," Twitter, November 17, 2012, 9:05 a.m., https://twitter.com/BillyGraham/status/269803413896826880 ; Billy Graham (@BillyGraham), "'When wealth is lost, nothing is lost; when health is lost, something is lost; when character is lost, all is lost.' #BillyGraham," Twitter, May 25, 2015, 9:03 a.m., https://twitter.com/billygraham/status/602822204296921088.

6. John C. Maxwell, *Success 101: What Every Leader Should Know* (New York: HarperCollins Leadership, 2008), 60.

7. Text generated by ChatGPT, OpenAI, https://chat.openai.com/chat.

8. Maxwell, *Success 101*, 60.

9. Tom Ziglar, *Choose to Win: Transform Your Life, One Simple Choice at a Time* (Nashville, TN: Nelson Books, 2021), 19.

10. Patrick Wrigley, "A Mystery on the Mountain of Pain," Roads and Kingdoms, November 25, 2014, https://roadsandkingdoms.com/2014/a-mystery-on-the-mountain-of-pain/

11. Aaditya Krishnamurthy, "Michael Jordan on His Best Skill: 'My Best Skill Was That I Was Coachable. I Was A Sponge And Aggressive To Learn.,'" Yardbarker, last updated January 3, 2022 https://bit.ly/4fnX1eN

12. Eben Pagan, *The Client-Getting Script: 11 Proven Words to Turn a Conversation Into a High-Paying Client* (self-pub, 2023), 30.

13. Luke 6:45 (New International Version).

14. Proverbs 4:23 (NIV).

15. Dr. James Kneller, "Can a Heart Transplant Change Your Personality?," JamesKnellerMD, July 14, 2021, YouTube video, 9:14, https://www.youtube.com/watch?v=dVwIm0VL5w8 Dr. Remi Nader, "'Cellular Memory' Heart Transplant Recipient and a Neurosurgeon Interview," Webivores, February 20, 2018, YouTube video, 9:08, https://www.youtube.com/watch?v=fn7qhAxPCKs

16. HeartMath Institute, "The Fascinating Relationship Between the Heart and Brain," November 21, 2021, YouTube video, 3:38, https://www.youtube.com/watch?v=WhxjXduD8qw

17. "The 'Little Brain in the Heart,'" HeartMath Institute, accessed May 5, 2024, https://www.heartmath.org/our-heart-brain/

18. Henry Ford, *My Life and Work* (New York: Garden City Publishing, 1922), 19–20.

19. Ryan Leak, *Chasing Failure: How Falling Short Sets You Up for Success* (Nashville, TN: W Publishing, 2021), 7.

20. Zig Ziglar, "Failure," Ziglar, accessed May 9, 2024, https://www.ziglar.com/quotes/failure-is-a-detour-not-a-dead-end-street/

21. John C. Maxwell, "Add Value to People," 12Stone Church, January 27, 2016, YouTube video, 2:24, https://www.youtube.com/watch?v=pIS9cxriits

22. Ken Blanchard (@kenblanchard), "I've always said, Feedback is the Breakfast of Champions. So are you a championship-level leader?" Twitter, March 8, 2022, https://twitter.com/kenblanchard/status/1501249552656990209?lang=en

23. Stephen R. Covey, *The 7 Habits of Highly Effective People: Powerful Lessons in Personal Change* (New York: Free Press, 2004).

24. John C. Maxwell, *Developing the Leader Within You* (New York: Thomas Nelson, 2005).

25. Mo Gawdat, "Mo Gawdat: AI Today, Tomorrow and How You Can Save Our World (Nordic Business Forum 2023)," *Slo Mo with Mo Gawdat*, October 2, 2023, YouTube video, 29:04, https://www.youtube.com/watch?v=u9CEUzH4HL4

26. Gawdat, "Mo Gawdat: AI Today."

27. John C. Maxwell, *Ethics 101: What Every Leader Needs to Know*, 101 Series (New York: Center Street, 2008), 15–16.

28. Maxwell, *Ethics 101*, 16.

29. Fred Kiel, *Return on Character: The Real Reason Leaders and Their Companies Win* (Boston: Harvard Business Review Press, 2015).

30. Myles Munroe, *Power of Character in Leadership: How Values, Morals, Ethics, and Principles Affect Leaders* (New Kensington: Whitaker House, 2017), 215.

31. Deutsch, *The Tricycle Effect*.

32. Zig Ziglar, *See You at the Top: 25th Anniversary Edition* (New Orleans: Pelican Publishing, 2000), 13.

33. Proverbs 5:22 (NIV).

34. John C. Maxwell, *Leadership Promises for Every Day: A Daily Devotional* (Nashville, TN: Thomas Nelson, 2007).

35. S.v. "mentor (*n.*)," Dictionary.com, accessed July 12, 2024, https://www.dictionary.com/browse/mentor.

36. Graham, "Integrity is the glue."; Graham, " 'When wealth is lost.' "

37. Maxwell, *The 21 Irrefutable Laws of Leadership*, 4.

38. *The Friend: A Religious and Literary Journal* 61, no. 7 (1888): 364.

39. Covey, *The 7 Habits of Highly Effective People*, 239.

40. Alexandra Silver, "Top 10 Twitter Controversies," *Time,* June 6, 2011, https://content.time.com/time/specials/packages/article/0,28804,2075071_2075082_2075112,00.html

41. Avshalom Caspi, "Three-Year-Old's Traits Predict Personality at Age 26," *Journal of Personality* 71, no. 4 (2003): 496–513, https://education-consumers.org/briefpdfs/4.7-childrens_behavior_age_3.pdf

42. "Six Pillars of Character," Character Counts, accessed May 12, 2024,

43. John C. Maxwell, *High Road Leadership: Bringing People Together in a World That Divides* (Maxwell Leadership, 2024).

44. Ford, *My Life and Work*, 19–20.

45. Ford, *My Life and Work.*

46. Leak, *Chasing Failure*, 7.

47. Chuck Carlson, *Game of My Life: 25 Stories of Packers Football* (Champaign, IL: Sports Publishing LLC, 2004), 149.

48. Ronald Reagan, "Remarks in Chicago, Illinois, at the Annual Convention and Centennial Observance of the United Brotherhood of Carpenters and Joiners," (speech, Chicago, IL, September 3, 1981) The American Presidency Project, accessed July 16, 2024, https://www.presidency.ucsb.edu/documents/remarks-chicago-illinois-the-annual-convention-and-centennial-observance-the-united

49. Henry Ford, "Quote Page," *Reader's Digest,* September 1947, 64.

50. John C. Maxwell, *Sometimes You Win, Sometimes You Learn: Life's Greatest Lessons Are Gained from Our Losses* (New York: Center Street, 2015), 28.

51. Carmine Gallo, "Four Communication Lessons I Learned from Real Top Gun Fighter Pilots," *Inc.,* May 25, 2022, https://www.inc.com/carmine-gallo/4-communication-lessons-i-learned-from-real-top-gun-fighter-pilots.html

52. Stephen R. Covey and Rebecca R. Merrill, *The Speed of Trust: The One Thing That Changes Everything* (New York: Free Press, 2018), 13.

53. Blanchard, "I've always said."

54. "Suffering from Imposter Syndrome? The Cure May Be Growth Mindset," March 18, 2021, NeuroLeadership Institute, https://neuroleadership.com/your-brain-at-work/imposter-syndrome-cure-growth-mindset/.

55. Christopher Sirk, "Xerox PARC and the Origins of GUI," CRM.Org, last updated January 23, 2024, https://crm.org/articles/xerox-parc-and-the-origins-of-gui

56. Scott Berkun, "How Skunkworks Got Its Name," Scott Berkun, July 13, 2006, https://scottberkun.com/2006/how-skunkworks-got-its-name-2/

57. Justin Thomas Miller, "The Butterfly Effect: How Small Changes Lead to Big Progress," Justin Thomas Miller, accessed May 5, 2024, https://justinthomasmiller.com/the-butterfly-effect-small-changes-lead-to-massive-progress

58. Ron Gutman, "The Hidden Power of Smiling | Ron Gutman," TED, May 11, 2011, YouTube video, 7:26, https://www.youtube.com/watch?v=U9cGdRNMdQQ

59. *Pinocchio,* directed by Norman Ferguson (1940; Burbank, CA: Walt Disney Productions, 1940).

60. Maxwell Maltz, *Psycho-Cybernetics* (New York: Simon & Schuster, 1960).

61. John C. Maxwell, *There's No Such Thing as "Business" Ethics: There's Only One Rule for Making Decisions* (New York: Center Street Publishing, 2003), 18.

62. Maxwell, *There's No Such Thing*, 4.

63. *The Mothers' Friend: A Monthly Magazine* 6, (London: Ward and Co., 1851), 38.

64. Noel M. Tichy and Warren G. Bennis, *Judgment: How Winning Leaders Make Great Calls* (New York: Penguin Publishing, 2009).

65. "FSU Gets Four Years Probation in Scandal," *Florida Times-Union*, March 6, 2009, https://www.jacksonville.com/story/sports/college/fsu-seminoles/2009/03/06/stub-179/15993797007/.

66. Robert H. Schuller, "Any fool can count the seeds in an apple, but only God can count the apples in one seed. God is constantly scattering seeds into our lives…" Facebook, September 19, 2011, https://www.facebook.com/100063715329593/posts/10150338747923905/

67. "Quote Page."

68. Maxwell, *The 21 Irrefutable Laws of Leadership*.

69. Michael T. Deane, "Top Six Reasons New Businesses Fail," Investopedia, last updated April 1, 2024, https://www.investopedia.com/financial-edge/1010/top-6-reasons-new-businesses-fail.aspx

70. Laurie Beth Jones, *Jesus, CEO: Using Ancient Wisdom for Visionary Leadership* (Westport, CT: Hyperion, 1996).

71. Tad Friend, "Jumpers," *New Yorker*, October 6, 2003, https://www.newyorker.com/magazine/2003/10/13/jumpers

72. Jon Acuff, *Soundtracks: The Surprising Solution to Overthinking* (Ada, Michigan: Baker Books, 2021), 35.

73. Acuff, *Soundtracks*, 57.

74. Acuff, *Soundtracks*,.

75. Acuff, *Soundtracks*, 34.

76. Acuff, *Soundtracks*, 31.

77. Kiel, *Return on Character*, 13.

78. "KRW Return on Character, Marketing ROC, Study Guide #4" (Lanesboro, MN: KRW International, 2021), 22.

79. Charles Duhigg, *The Power of Habit: Why We Do What We Do in Life and Business*, 10th anniversary ed. (New York: Random House, 2023), 19.

80. "KRW Return on Character, What Is Character, Study Guide #1" (Lanesboro, MN: KRW International, 2021).

81. Duhigg, *The Power of Habit*, 19.

82. "KRW Return on Character, What Is Character, Study Guide #1," 11.

83. Kendra Cherry, "What Is the Negativity Bias?," VeryWell Mind, last updated November 13, 2023, https://www.verywellmind.com/negative-bias-4589618.

84. "The Impact of Negative Thoughts and How to Process Them," The Waltline Group, last updated June 11, 2020, https://thewaltlinegroup.com/the-impact-of-negative-thoughts-and-how-to-process-them

85. Blanchard (@kenblanchard), "I've always said."

86. Jim Collins, "BHAG," Jim Collins, accessed May 12, 2024, https://www.jimcollins.com/concepts/bhag.html

87. Corrie Ten Boom, *Jesus Is Victor* (Tarrytown: New York, 1973), 184.

88. Zig Ziglar, *Life Wisdom: Quotes from Zig Ziglar* (Nashville, TN: Meadow's Edge Group LLC, 2014), 64.

89. Maxwell, *High Road Leadership*.

90. Dave Anderson, "Courage and Defeating Your Fears," *Leader of Character*, April 15, 2024, Vimeo video, 1:11, https://vimeo.com/934950434?share=copy

91. Maxwell, *High Road Leadership*.

92. Lewis Howes, "Do This to Cut Out Negativity from Your Life | Price Pritchett," Greatness Clips – Lewis Howes, November 30, 2023, YouTube video, 10:19, https://www.youtube.com/watch?v=SDeGGA9Bvtw

93. Jason N. Linder, "Hacking the Brain's Negative Bias," *Mindfulness Insights* (blog), Psychology Today, May 8, 2021, https://www.psychologytoday.com/us/blog/mindfulness-insights/202105/hacking-the-brains-negative-bias

94. Eric Hepburn, "The Seven Times Distortion: Negativity Bias Reconsidered," Medium, June 14, 2023, https://ericdhepburn.medium.com/the-7x-distortion-negativity-bias-reconsidered-2456ab56e677

95. Saman Javed, "Negative Social Media Posts Get Twice as Much Engagement Than Positive Ones, Study Finds," *Independent*, June 22, 2021, https://www.independent.co.uk/life-style/social-media-facebook-twitter-politics-b1870628.html

96. Jacob Hornik et al., "Information Dissemination Via Electronic Word-of-Mouth: Good News Travels Fast, Bad News Travels Faster!," *Computers in Human Behavior* 45 (April 2015): 273–280, https://doi.org/10.1016/j.chb.2014.11.008 ; Cherry, "Negativity Bias."

97. Soroush Vosoughi, Deb Roy, and Sinan Aral, "The Spread of True and False News Online," *Science* 359, no. 6380 (2018): 1146–1151, https://doi.org/10.1126/science.aap9559 .

98. Jacob Hornik et al., "Information Dissemination Via Electronic Word-of-Mouth."

99. 2 Corinthians 10:5 (NIV).

100. Maxwell, *The 21 Irrefutable Laws of Leadership.*

www.ingramcontent.com/pod-product-compliance
Lightning Source LLC
LaVergne TN
LVHW021756060526
838201LV00058B/3110